Contents

Europe's blurred boundaries

Rethinking enlargement and neighbourhood policy

Charles Grant

ABOUT THE AUTHOR

Charles Grant has been director of the Centre for European Reform since he helped to found it in 1998. Previously he worked as a journalist for *Euromoney* and *The Economist*. He is the author of 'Delors: Inside the House that Jacques built' (Nicholas Brealey, 1994) and numerous CER publications including 'Transatlantic rift: how to bring the two sides together' (2003) and 'What happens if Britain votes no?' (2005).

AUTHOR'S ACKNOWLEDGEMENTS

I would like to thank those who have read and commented on drafts, as well as those who have been kind enough to discuss the pamphlet's ideas. I owe particular thanks to Ian Boag, Robert Cooper, Markus Ederer, Steven Everts, Michael Leigh, Mark Leonard, Chris Patten, Olli Rehn, Jean Pisani-Ferry, Pirkka Tapiola, Simon Tilford, Aurore Wanlin and Rutger Wissels. Katinka Barysch, Hugo Brady and Heather Grabbe have been especially helpful. Thanks to Kate Meakins for layout and production.

I would like to thank the German Marshall Fund of the United States for supporting the CER's work on enlargement and neighbourhood policy. I would also like to thank the Open Society Institute for sponsoring this pamphlet.

Foreword

 OPEN SOCIETY INSTITUTE

European integration has been a driving force for peace, democratisation, stability and prosperity in Europe. The visionary ideas and actions of post-war politicians have transformed a continent that only 60 years ago was torn by conflict and war into a peaceful one which successfully promotes democracy, human rights, the rule of law and a functioning market economy. These are the values that characterise an open society. The European Union has done more than any other actor to spread them – not only through words, but also by providing a clear model for developing open societies and the necessary assistance to enshrine these values. The countries of Central and Eastern Europe would not have developed into the open societies they are now without the incentives and guidance of EU integration.

The introduction of referendums into European politics has made public support vital for the future expansion of the EU. In the short term, the gap in opinion between political elites and the European public has jeopardised popular support for further European integration. However, the setback can be overcome if European leaders take this challenge as an opportunity to make an effective case for further internal and external integration to the citizens of the EU.

The Open Society Institute is not a promoter of European integration per se, but we regard it as a tried and tested model for building sustainable open societies. It is in the interest of both the current EU member-states and the countries that aspire to join to keep the perspective of integration open to all European countries. Closing that door will deprive the EU of its most successful foreign policy instrument.

This CER pamphlet discusses the challenges for further European integration and proposes concrete ideas to make enlargement viable for members, potential members and EU neighbours, without diluting current standards. As we welcome open debate about the issue of European integration and its challenges, we are very happy to be associated with this discussion paper.

Mabel van Oranje, Director EU Affairs, Open Society Institute

Andre Wilkens, Director, Open Society Institute-Brussels

1 Introduction: The EU's malaise

For the past several years, the words 'European Union' and 'crisis' have been inextricably linked. And yet, despite all the negative news tied to the Union – such as budget rows, lost referendums and economic under-performance – it is an organisation that continues to notch up real achievements. Since 1999 the EU has launched a single currency; taken in ten new members; introduced a common arrest warrant to speed up cross-border extradition; continued to deepen the single market in areas such as financial services and energy; created an (admittedly imperfect) emissions trading scheme to curb the output of greenhouse gases; forged common foreign policies for dealing with problems such as Iran; developed co-operation on defence that is keeping the peace in places like Bosnia; and done much else.

Nevertheless, the EU is suffering from a malaise, one which threatens to slow down or prevent any further enlargement of the Union. This malaise stems from the mixing together of at least four distinct problems.

★ The poor performance of the core euroland economies has made many people fearful of change, whether it comes in the form of new EU treaties or fresh rounds of enlargement. In many EU countries, the Union now symbolises the forces of globalisation. It is viewed – with some justice – as the body that tries to remove the barriers to trade and the free movement of people across an increasingly wide area. As a consequence, those who see globalisation as a threat to their jobs, or believe that there are too many immigrants in their country, tend to hold the EU responsible. A lot of people see the EU as a source of insecurity rather than as a resource to help governments soften the pains provoked by globalisation.

★ The failure of the constitutional treaty has left a cloud of uncertainty hanging over the EU's institutions. Although the European public cares little about institutions and treaty changes, many politicians and officials see that the EU's institutional structure is seriously flawed. Yet there is no consensus on either the institutional reforms required, or the best method for negotiating and then implementing a reform package. The fact that there is little immediate prospect of improving decision-making procedures makes many politicians and officials extremely reluctant to contemplate further EU enlargement.

★ Partly as a consequence of those economic and institutional problems, the legitimacy of the EU has diminished among broad sections of the European public. As the EU has expanded, becoming increasingly diverse, the sense of common purpose among its member-states has diminished. The number of people considering EU membership 'a good thing' has been falling in all large member-states, and at the end of 2005 stood at just 50 per cent in the 'EU-15' (those countries already in the Union before May 2004). Many Europeans see the EU institutions as remote, complex and hard to understand, but few are aware of the many practical benefits they deliver. So long as the Union itself suffers from a popularity problem, the idea of enlarging it is also likely to be unpopular.

★ All these problems are compounded by a leadership vacuum: the Commission's authority is weak, while many member-states have leaders who appear to care little about the fate of the European Union. They frequently use the EU as a scapegoat, as when French politicians blame the Commission for failing to prevent job losses in France. Leaders have done little to explain the benefits of the Union in general, or enlargement in particular. A recent Eurobarometer survey reveals a correlation between the level of information people have about enlargement and support for the policy. In the 25 member-states, 68 per cent of people say

they are not well informed about enlargement. In France, one of
the members most hostile to a wider EU, only 10 per cent say
they are well informed about the benefits   [1] *'Attitudes to European Union*
of enlargement, while 54 per cent say   *enlargement', Eurobarometer,*
they know about the problems associated   *July 2006.*
with the policy.[1]

The EU's malaise means that two of its defining characteristics over
the past 20 years – continual 'deepening' through treaty-based
integration, and continual 'widening' through the accession of new
members – can no longer be taken for granted. This has big
implications for the countries in the EU's neighbourhood – both those
that aspire to join in the next few years, and those further afield.

The EU's neighbourhood consists mainly of countries trying to cope
with serious problems, such as high unemployment, extreme
poverty, ethnic tension, political instability and organised crime. In
fact, an arc of instability surrounds the EU, stretching from Belarus
to Ukraine to Moldava to the Western Balkans to the Caucasus to
the Middle East to North Africa. A truism that needs to be repeated
is that the EU cannot afford to turn its back on this neighbourhood.
Unless the EU redoubles its efforts to promote stability, security,
prosperity and good governance in these countries, it risks paying a
heavy price. It may have to cope with boatloads of economic
migrants, fight gangs of organised criminals entering the EU, shelter
swarms of refugees from civil wars and ethnic conflicts, or despatch
battalions of soldiers to keep the peace in conflict zones.

The EU needs to take a two-pronged approach to its
neighbourhood. Those countries that are geographically close and
European require a clear perspective of membership. The other
neighbours should be offered a strong European neighbourhood
policy that, though lacking the goal of full membership, brings
them much closer to the EU. This pamphlet will argue that the
EU's malaise makes the first of those objectives more difficult, and
the second more urgent.

Many critics of enlargement claim that it has accentuated the EU's problems. Thus some populists blame Europe's economic woes on the cost of enlargement, now that large sums of aid go to East European farmers and regions; on the practice of *délocalisation*, whereby companies shift factories from Western Europe to Eastern Europe; and on immigrants from the east taking jobs in Western Europe.

Others accuse enlargement of damaging the efficiency of EU institutions. For example, now that the Council of Ministers has expanded from 15 to 25 government, its ability to take decisions smoothly and effectively has – it is claimed – been damaged.

I will argue below that the first accusation is false: enlargement has in fact strengthened the EU economy, rather than weakened it. And the second claim, that enlargement has disrupted the institutions, is an exaggeration, though the arrival of ten new members in May 2004 has led to some difficulties.

Two further criticisms have a greater basis in fact. Enlargement is said to have worsened the EU's legitimacy problem. To the extent that a wider EU embraces a broad array of peoples and cultures, with which some West Europeans may feel little in common, enlargement may weaken the sense of community which helps to bind the EU together. And for those worried about globalisation and neo-liberalism, enlargement has made the EU less appealing: many of the new member-states tend to support liberalisation and oppose Europe-wide social standards.

One other criticism contains a grain of truth: according to its critics, enlargement has worsened the leadership problem. A larger and more diverse organisation evidently requires more skilled leadership than a small and cohesive club. The Franco-German duo, which used to steer the Union, cannot do so when there are 25 members. However, the dearth of effective leadership, though a problem today, was just as evident before the May 2004 enlargement. Leadership is a problem whatever the number of member-states.

This pamphlet looks at the impact of the EU's malaise on the prospect of further enlargement. It analyses the reasons why governments and voters in some parts of Europe have become more hostile to a broader EU, and suggests ways of overcoming this hostility. It argues that an extension of the principle of 'variable geometry', the idea that small groups of member-states should integrate more closely in certain policy areas, could make enlargement more palatable for some doubters. The pamphlet considers the merits of the 'European neighbourhood policy', the EU's tool for dealing with neighbours that have no immediate prospect of becoming candidates for membership. Then it proposes new and closer forms of association for such countries.

The conclusion is that in the long run, 'membership' of the EU will mean different things for different countries, with some becoming more integrated into *avant-garde* groups than others; and that the difference between the rights and privileges enjoyed by EU members and some non-members is likely to blur.

The EU and its neighbourhood

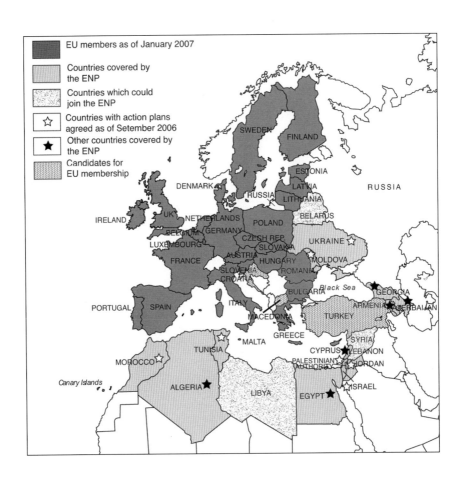

2 Europe turns against enlargement

Ever since the 1970s, there has been a close link between 'deepening', the movement towards a more politically integrated EU, and 'widening', the enlargement of the Union. Political elites in countries such as France have always been reluctant to widen the EU, believing that a larger Union could not easily evolve into the 'political union' they desire. They feared that the British wanted enlargement in order to fulfil the Thatcherite dream of an EU that was little more than a glorified free trade area, with weaker institutions and a diminished sense of solidarity. A wider Europe, of course, would also dilute the influence of France, Germany and the Benelux countries.

But despite these reservations, the EU has continued to enlarge – in 1981, 1986, 1995 and 2004. Those sceptical of enlargement, including many federalists and the French, swallowed their doubts. They did so because they extracted a price: a series of treaties that created a more integrated Europe – those negotiated in 1985, 1991, 1997, 2000 and finally the constitutional treaty, signed in 2004 but unlikely to ever enter into force. The British, Scandinavians and some other enthusiasts for enlargement were never particularly keen on treaty-based integration, but accepted it as the quid pro quo of the widening they wanted.

The Germans sat in the middle of this debate. They have favoured deepening, because of their generally federalist approach to the EU. They have viewed a more united Europe as serving the German national interest. But Germany has also favoured enlargement – especially the expansion into Eastern Europe – as a means of promoting stability and prosperity in its immediate neighbourhood.

Many Germans saw enlargement as a way of dealing with their country's traumatic historical relationship with neighbours such as Poland. German companies also had much to gain from the extension of the single market into Germany's hinterland.

The Commission, like Germany, has traditionally been pro-deepening and pro-widening. Pro-deepening, because the Commission is likely to have a larger role to play in a more integrated Europe. And pro-widening because it sees that a bigger EU has the potential to wield more global influence (and, some cynics would say, because it gets to run the accession talks).

[2] *Gideon Rachman, 'The death of enlargement', Washington Quarterly, Summer 2006.* The Commission also understands that deepening and widening reinforce each other.[2] The Thatcherite belief that a wider Europe would be shallower has – at least until now – proved to be wrong. The accession of Britain was followed by the creation of structural funds. After Greece, Spain and Portugal joined, the Union built the single market and planned the monetary union. Soon after Austria, Finland and Sweden joined, the EU started to get serious about foreign and defence policy.

For much of the past dozen years, the prospect of enlargement into Eastern Europe has made governments think they should strengthen EU institutions through treaty change; they have worried that a wider EU might become ungovernable. Thus enlargement was a big influence on the inter-governmental conferences (IGCs) that sought to revise the treaties in 1996-97, 2000 and 2003-04. Conversely, the succession of treaty revisions between 1985 and 2004 gave governments the confidence to think about extending the EU not only into Eastern Europe but also towards the Balkans and Turkey.

This implicit bargain between deepeners and wideners has driven the EU forward for the past 20 years. The demise of the constitutional treaty has therefore done much more than bring an end to treaty-based integration for the foreseeable future: it has also created major obstacles to further enlargement of the EU.

In Germany, for example, there has been a notable shift of opinion against enlargement. In the summer of 2005, just after the French and Dutch referendums, when Germans were asked whether they would prefer deeper co-operation among existing members, or further enlargement, 84 per cent said they would choose deeper co-operation, and 6 per cent enlargement. The share of those choosing deeper co-operation had risen by almost ten percentage points from a year earlier.[3]

[3] 'Allensbacher Berichte', Institut für Demoskopie Allensbach, June 2005.

The climate for enlargement was deteriorating even before the French and Dutch referendums. France had changed its constitution in March 2005 so that any country wishing to join after Bulgaria, Romania and Croatia cannot do so without a positive referendum in France. This constitutional change was in part an attempt to remove the issue of Turkish accession from the referendum campaign on the constitutional treaty. But it did not succeed. In France – and in the Netherlands – some of those voting No did so because they opposed Turkish membership, although formally the treaty had nothing to do with Turkey. Another reason why French people voted No to the constitutional treaty was to protest against the 2004 enlargement, which had been unpopular in France. (There were of course many other reasons for the French *Non*, including dislike of President Chirac, fears that the EU's liberalising services directive would increase job insecurity, and a general view that the EU was moving too far in a neo-liberal and Anglo-Saxon direction.)

Public support for the concept of enlargement peaked in 2001 but has been dropping ever since – a fall that has coincided with a gloomy economic situation in many parts of the EU. In Germany, France and Austria, six out of ten people are now against any new countries joining the EU (though among all 25 EU members, only 39 per cent oppose any further enlargement). Among the EU-25, 43 per cent of people oppose Ukrainian membership (with 42 per cent in favour), 44 per cent oppose Serbian membership (with 39 per cent in favour), 50 per cent oppose Albanian membership (with 33 per cent in favour), and 55 per cent oppose Turkish membership (with 31 per cent in favour).[4]

[4] 'The future of Europe',
Eurobarometer, May 2006.

For many Europeans, the recent enlargement looks like a 'mini-globalisation', because it has added around 40 million low-cost workers to the EU labour market. Indeed, the countries which most fear globalisation tend to be those most opposed to further EU enlargement. There is also quite a strong correlation between the countries which are hostile to enlargement and those which suffer from low economic growth and high unemployment.[5]

[5] Austria is an exception.
Despite its low unemployment,
the boom in Austrian investment
in the new member-states, and
soaring trade between Austria
and its neighbours, its public
opinion is strongly
anti-enlargement.

There is no doubt that the French and Dutch referendums have darkened the prospect of a much wider Europe. Since the referendums, several leading French politicians – including Nicolas Sarkozy, Dominique de Villepin and Laurent Fabius – have increased their hostility to Turkish accession. So have Edmund Stoiber and other senior German Christian Democrats (though Angela Merkel, having previously spoken out strongly against Turkish membership, has said very little in 2006). Austrian leaders have been especially hostile to Turkey, almost vetoing the opening of accession talks in October 2005.

In many countries, senior officials, politicians and pundits are arguing that the EU should not expand into the Balkans, Turkey or elsewhere until and unless it can strengthen its institutions. In March 2006 the European Parliament passed a resolution on enlargement, recalling that "the capacity for absorption of the Union, as set out in the 1993 Copenhagen European Council, remains one of the conditions for the accession of new countries....The stalemate in the ratification of the treaty establishing a constitution for Europe is preventing the Union from enhancing its absorption capacity." Elmar Brok MEP, the *rapporteur* on that resolution, and many other MEPs, regard it as self-evident that no further enlargement can take place until the institutional crisis is resolved, preferably through salvaging the bulk of the constitution. No candidate can join the EU without a positive vote on its accession treaty in the European Parliament.

Increasingly, those hostile to further enlargement are stressing the importance of the EU's 'absorption capacity'. They believe that by shifting the enlargement debate from its usual focus on the preparedness of applicants to cope with the EU, to the preparedness of the EU to cope with new members, they will persuade more people to favour a halt. An unofficial French government paper circulating in June 2006 defined absorption capacity as three things: the state of public opinion in the member-states; the strength of the EU institutions; and the capacity of the EU's policies and financial resources to cope with further accessions.

Some of that thinking appeared in the conclusions of the June 2006 European Council. These said that the "pace of enlargement must take the Union's absorption capacity into account". The European Council asked the Commission to draw up a special report on the Union's absorption capacity. This should "cover the issue of present and future perceptions of enlargement by citizens and should take into account the need to explain the enlargement process adequately to the public within the Union".

Seen one way, that is a perfectly reasonable suggestion: of course Europe's leaders should take account of public opinion when it is hostile to enlargement, so that they are motivated to do a better job of selling EU expansion. Seen another way, those words could mean that no applicant should be allowed to join if public opinion is broadly hostile. Many candidate countries fear the latter interpretation.

3   The pros and cons of further enlargement

During 2006, in France, Germany and elsewhere, there has been talk of the EU defining its ultimate boundaries. "Fixing a geographical and political framework for the Union is an essential precondition for our citizens to identify once again with the European project", says Nicholas Sarkozy, leader of France's Gaullists. "We must now say who is European and who is not – it is no longer possible to avoid this question."[6] Sarkozy would take in Iceland, Norway, Switzerland and the Balkan states – when they are ready – but no other country.

6 Nicholas Sarkozy, speech to Friends of Europe, Brussels, September 8th 2006.

However, any such attempt to draw an indelible line on the map would be unwise. The EU should maintain an open door for countries that wish to join, so long as they are clearly European, or at least can present a case that they are; and so long as they meet the EU's criteria for accession, strictly interpreted. (Some countries close to the EU cannot claim to be European: those of North Africa, the Middle East and Central Asia.)

Nevertheless, there are respectable arguments for opposing enlargement or saying that it should proceed only very slowly. These include the effect of enlargement on EU institutions; the readiness of the candidates; and the impact on the EU labour market. Advocates of enlargement have not always paid sufficient attention to these arguments.

The effect of enlargement on EU institutions

Each new member of the EU imposes additional strains and stresses on an institutional system that was designed for six countries and finds coping with 25 difficult. Of course, successive treaty changes have led to modest reforms to the institutions and decision-making procedures. Overall, however, the system does not work particularly well. Hence the effort to draft the constitutional treaty, a compromise document which ultimately won the signatures of all 25 governments in June 2004, though French and Dutch electors subsequently voted it down.

The demise of that treaty means that, for the time being, the EU cannot make big changes to its institutions. Meanwhile, the arrival of ten new members in May 2004 – the most extensive enlargement in the EU's history – is starting to make an impact on the way the Union works. Writing only two years after that accession, it is too soon to judge the long-term consequences, but some are already apparent.

The consequences for decision-making

The experience of the past two years suggests that the current institutional framework can more or less cope with a 25-country Union. The new members have not often disrupted business by wielding their vetoes – though Cyprus has blocked the EU from opening up trade with Northern Cyprus, while Poland held up a deal on VAT (before eventually climbing down).

In an interesting article on absorption capacity, Frank Vibert attacks the concept, making the case that the EU can happily continue to enlarge with its current institutions. He argues that the EU is not a club whose benefits become diluted if more members join. "Many of the benefits of EU membership flow from common rules, whose value increases as more people subscribe to them. The benefits are 'network' benefits that increase with size and not – as the 'absorption capacity' model has it – benefits based on sharing out something with a fixed supply."[7]

[7] *Frank Vibert, 'Absorption capacity: the wrong European debate', Open Democracy, June 2006.*

That point is correct. But Vibert's analysis is ultimately too Panglossian, for he says nothing about the practical effect of enlargement on the Council of Ministers. When the Council expanded from 15 to 25 governments, its role as a forum for hammering out decisions declined. Governments now tend to use the Council as the place where they state their positions, leaving the real deals to be made by smaller groups elsewhere. Ministers, especially those from larger countries, often skip some or all of Council meetings, relying on deputies or officials to represent them. Meetings of ministerial councils that used to last for a day now sometimes endure for a day and a half. In theory *tours de table*, the system whereby every minister speaks in turn, have been scrapped, but in practice nearly every government wants to talk on the big questions.

"Ecofin [the finance ministers' council] takes decisions more slowly, not because ministers wield vetoes, but because of the time it takes for everyone to have their say," observes Caio Koch-Weser, who was Germany's deputy finance minister in the Schröder government. "There are more member-states who have problems that the presidency has to sort out."

Observers of the General Affairs and External Relations Council (that of the foreign ministers) tell a similar story. "Decisions at ministerial or official level take longer – sometimes there is no decision at all, because the effort of constructing a consensus is too great, and sometimes the quality of the decision is very lowest common denominator," notes one Council official. When Russia is on the agenda, two factions try to steer the Council in opposing directions. The 'pro-Russian' camp of France, Germany and Italy competes against the 'anti-Russian' camp of the Baltic states, Poland and other East Europeans. The result is that anything which comes out of the Council on Russia tends to be extremely bland.

This problem of slow decision-making affects meetings of officials as much as ministers. In Coreper (the committee of member-states' EU ambassadors), which plays a key role in EU decision-making, representatives are now more prone to read out prepared statements, which means they have to stick more closely to their governments' positions; there is less scope for manoeuvre and informal compromise.

Thus, enlargement does appear to have made an impact, but it is worth remembering that several other factors also influence the speed of decision-taking. One is the overall political climate in the European Union: acrimony slows things down. Another is the quality of leadership – in the rotating presidency, national capitals and the Commission.

The consequences for the balance between large and small countries

One potentially damaging effect of enlargement has been to alter the balance of power between large and small countries. Of those joining in May 2004, Poland is a large country, but the other nine are small (none having more than 10 million people). The EU's decision-making system has always given an advantage to small countries in the Council, through voting weights that are disproportionate to their populations, under the qualified majority voting system, and through veto rights that are identical to those enjoyed by large countries. The small countries have also benefited from over-representation in the European Parliament, relative to their populations; and from every member-state being entitled to both a commissioner and a judge in the European Court of Justice. The bias in favour of smaller member-states caused few problems when there were roughly equal numbers of large and small ones, for the large countries proved skilful at ensuring that their interests were taken into account.

[8] Under double majority voting, a measure would pass if 55 per cent of the member-states were in favour, so long as they represented 65 per cent of the Union's people.

The constitutional treaty was, among other things, an attempt to find a compromise between the interests of large and small countries. The creation of a full-time EU president, at the expense of the rotating presidency; the introduction of a fair and simple voting system, 'double majority voting'[8]; and the creation of an EU foreign minister, all promoted – or were perceived as promoting – large countries' interests. However, the provision on the number of commissioners, perhaps the most strange and ill-conceived element in the treaty, did the opposite.

The Nice treaty says that the formula of one commissioner per country should continue until there are 27 member-states. When that number is reached the European Council should decide on a new system that brings the number of commissioners below 27. The negotiations on the constitutional treaty sought to deal with the number of commissioners in advance of Bulgaria's and Romania's accession, since their entry will take the membership to 27. The large countries wanted to cut the numbers of commissioners, for the sake of a more efficient college; but the small countries would not agree to a cut without a rotation system that treated all countries equally. The constitutional treaty therefore lays down a procedure under which countries take turns not to have a commissioner. This system could conceivably lead to a situation in which Britain or Germany or France or Italy had no commissioner, but Bosnia, Croatia, Kosovo, Macedonia, Montenegro, Serbia and Slovenia each had one.

Such a farcical scenario would in fact be highly unlikely: the details of the rotation would probably include an element of geographical balance. However, any system of appointing commissioners that treated large and small members identically would be guaranteed to alienate the largest ones from the Commission in particular and the EU in general. The Commission cannot work effectively without the support of most of the large countries, as was evident during the first year of the Barroso Commission, when President Chirac and Chancellor Schröder treated President José Manuel Barroso with contempt. Therefore, in the coming negotiations on treaties and institutional reform, the governments must be careful to ensure a sensible balance between the interests of large and small countries.

Small countries need to realise that, as the EU expands, it is becoming harder to convince large member-states that they should act formally through EU institutions rather than in small informal groups. "Small countries need to be very careful not to become too attached to points of principle in protecting their interests," says Professor Loukas Tsoukalis, president of Greece's Eliamep think-tank. "Otherwise they may drive the large countries to work outside the EU." And if large member-states ignore EU institutions, small ones tend to be disadvantaged.

This imbalance between big and small countries will grow, assuming that the EU continues to enlarge. While Romania, with 20 million people, can count as a middle-sized country, Bulgaria and all the Western Balkan states are small. The prospect of the likes of Montenegro and Macedonia having their own commissioners and wielding a veto in the Council of Ministers is enough to turn many people off enlargement – and not only in the larger member-states.

So to ensure a balance between the interests of large and small, the EU should adopt the double majority voting system as soon as possible. In areas that remain subject to unanimity, the smaller member-states should be careful to use their veto powers only sparingly. And when it comes to numbers of commissioners, the smaller members should accept one of two systems: either every state would continue to have its own commissioner – but some of them, and not those from the large countries, would be 'junior commissioners'; or there would be a system of rotation that privileged large countries, with the smaller countries taking turns to stand down from the Commission. My guess is that the second model would be unacceptable to some small countries.

With the EU's membership soon rising to 27, only those who care nothing for the effectiveness of the Union will argue that it should undertake another significant round of enlargement before making major institutional reforms.

Proponents of enlargement need to show that the EU's policies and institutions can function effectively with an increased membership. British politicians are often the most ardent advocates of enlargement. But because they tend to assume that the EU can continue enlarging without major reforms of its institutions and decision-making procedures, their views are often discounted in other countries. Many senior continental European politicians who favour further enlargement – such as Commission President Barroso, former German foreign minister Joschka Fischer, and former French Europe minister Pierre Moscovici – are adamant that without major changes to the treaties the EU should not and will not take in more countries.

The readiness of the candidates

A second reason for taking a cautious attitude to further widening is concern over the readiness of the candidate countries. Accession would almost certainly have a beneficial impact on them. But would the economies and political systems of the candidates enable them to act as constructive members within the Union? Would their governments be capable of administering EU funds and enforcing EU rules? Given the importance of the principle of the mutual recognition of court decisions to EU judicial co-operation, could their legal systems be trusted to play fair? Would the new members be able to offer positive contributions to the existing member-states or to EU policies, for example by providing well-regulated markets for exports and investments, skilled workers, expertise on problematic neighbours, or soldiers and policemen for EU missions?

So far, the judicial systems of the ten new members seem to be coping quite well. For example, early in 2006, a Pole accused of murdering a youth in Brussels, who had fled to Poland, was quickly sent back to Belgium for trial. The European arrest warrant worked.

The Commission has particular concerns about corruption in Bulgaria and Romania, and the effectiveness of their judicial systems. In 2004 the Commission was reluctant to give this pair a date for accession, on the grounds that they needed to carry out a raft of reforms before they were ready. But a clumsy political fix led to the Commission being over-ruled. President Jacques Chirac insisted on Bulgaria and Romania being given a date, for reasons that are not entirely clear. The European Council went along with this – perhaps out of gratitude for Bulgaria and Romania supporting NATO's military action against Serbia in 1999, despite the collateral damage inflicted on their economies. The result was a foolish and irrational decision, that they would join in 2007 or 2008, whether or not they had fulfilled their promises on reform. Thus the EU weakened its leverage over these two countries.

Bulgaria and Romania are likely to be problematic members, at least in their first few years in the Union. In June 2006 a report from the EU's Court of Auditors said that up to half the €1.9 billion of EU aid given to Bulgaria and Romania between 2000 and 2004 had been poorly spent. For example, a bridge built over the River Prut between Romania and Moldova could not be used for several years because there was no road on the Moldovan side. An international conference centre in Constanta, Romania, was abandoned half-built because the county council withdrew its construction permit. And a post-privatisation investment fund in Bulgaria, set up jointly by the Commission and the European Bank for Reconstruction and Development, proved a disaster: before being wound up it had invested just €11.6 million in six companies (€4 million of which went to one company that folded), though the fund managers and their advisers had been paid €4.5 million. The report blamed lack of administrative capacity in the recipient countries, as well as poor selection of projects by the Commission.

Let us hope that Bulgaria and Romania make rapid progress to justify the confidence that has been placed in them. But if they do not, and if they appear to lack the capacity to administer EU policies and programmes, and if stories emerge of organised crime benefiting from EU funds, the whole process of enlargement will be thrown into disrepute.

The accession of Bulgaria and Romania in January 2007 will not be the first occasion the EU has been over-hasty in letting in new members. For example, until the early 1990s, it was often said in Brussels – including by Commission President Jacques Delors – that it had been a mistake to let in Greece in 1981. In the late 1970s the then French president, Valéry Giscard d'Estaing, overturned the Commission's view that Greece was not ready and the EU began accession talks with it. For more than a decade after it joined, the forceful nationalism of the Greek government was prone to disrupt the workings of the EU (sometimes in partnership with the nationalism of Thatcherite Britain). The corruption of the Greek administration led to much of the EU money spent in Greece being wasted. But then in the mid-1990s the country underwent a transformation, and Greece has now become a valued and constructive member of the club.

Today, many senior Brussels officials and commissioners say that it was a mistake to let in Cyprus in 2004, without an agreement on how to overcome the island's division. In its first two years as a member, Cyprus does not appear to have learned that members enhance their influence by making allies, moderating their nationalism and acting in a spirit of compromise. Since the Law and Justice government took office in Warsaw in October 2005, Poland has sometimes seemed to be competing with Cyprus for the title of the Union's most obstreperous member. In the long run, hopefully, Cyprus and Poland will undergo the same sort of positive transformation experienced by Greece.

As far as future accessions are concerned, if a new member were to bring into the EU a fierce and uncompromising strain of nationalism, the forging of compromises in the Council of Ministers could become much harder. The Copenhagen accession criteria do not include any formal requirement for a candidate's politicians to moderate their nationalism. But the Western Balkans does host some of the continent's rawest and most potent forms of nationalism, as the wars of the 1990s revealed. The EU must leave the door open to the Western Balkan states. But it should also make clear to them that preparing for membership means learning to be 'post-modern', in the sense of understanding that supranational institutions will constrain their governments' freedom of manoeuvre; and in the sense of accepting that the EU's philosophy is to overcome conflict through peaceful negotiation and compromise.[9] Given that many EU decisions do – and for the foreseeable future, will – require unanimity, it would be disastrous for the EU to admit any state that has not got that message. That applies to the Balkan states, to Turkey and any others that wish to join.

[9] The idea of the 'post-modern' state is developed by Robert Cooper in 'The breaking of nations', Atlantic Books, 2003.

Clearly, there are lessons to be drawn from earlier and current enlargements. Countries should not be allowed in if they have unresolved border disputes with their neighbours. In helping candidates to prepare for membership, the EU should place a greater emphasis on good governance. The EU should not grant a candidate a precise date at which its entry is guaranteed. And it should be in no hurry to admit a country that seems prone to atavistic nationalism.

The two reasons for caution presented so far in this chapter – worries about the institutional equilibrium of the Union, and the readiness of the candidates – matter for insiders, such as politicians, journalists and academics. But they are not the main driver of popular opposition to further enlargement, to which the argument now turns.

The impact of enlargement on labour markets

The reasons for popular hostility to enlargement vary from country to country. In France, the Netherlands, Austria and Germany, there is a particular antipathy to the idea of Muslim countries in the EU, and thus to Turkish accession. In France EU enlargement is unpopular because it has, with some justice, been seen as a cause of the country's declining political, cultural and linguistic influence in the Union. If anyone had asked the French to vote in a referendum on the May 2004 enlargement, the result probably would have been a resounding *Non*. Countries that are close to potential members tend to favour their accession, but those more distant tend to be hostile. Thus Poland and Lithuania would like to see Ukraine (and maybe one day Belarus) in the Union, but few other members agree. As soon as Romania is in the EU it will bang a drum for its neighbour Moldova, probably without gaining much support from fellow members.

One common thread running through opposition to enlargement in many parts of the Union is fear of free movement of labour. This is not an irrational or silly fear. The introduction of free movement of labour between a current member and a would-be member would create economic gains in both countries, overall, but disadvantage some people in the current member-state.

In 2003, 43 per cent of people in the EU-15 feared that enlargement would push up unemployment in their country. In 2006, that figure had risen to 63 per cent. In Germany, the country which received the most East European workers before the May 2004 enlargement, the figure jumped from 56 per cent to 80 per cent over those three years. In France 72 per cent and in Austria 75 per cent fear that enlargement threatens their jobs (even in the UK, the figure is 64 per cent).[10]

[10] Eurobarometer, 'The future of Europe', May 2006.

Of the 15 older member-states, only Britain, Ireland and Sweden allowed East Europeans unrestricted access to their labour markets after May 2004. In the summer of 2006, Finland, Greece, Italy, Portugal and Spain followed suit, while France and several other members ended restrictions on certain categories of worker. Britain, Ireland and Sweden had relatively low levels of unemployment and even labour shortages in some sectors. Around 600,000 Central and East Europeans have come to Britain, working in areas such as hotels, catering, child-care, cleaning, agriculture and public transport, without provoking a great deal of hostility or disruption. Well over 100,000 turned up in much smaller Ireland, seeking similar sorts of job, and causing a greater political stir. These influxes have undoubtedly held down wage rates for local people working in the sectors affected, though the overall economic impact has been highly beneficial, contributing to strong economic growth.

High-unemployment countries like France or Germany could not so easily have opened their doors in this way. Their economies would have gained from the arrival of hard-working, productive immigrants, but at a possible price of growing xenophobia among those who saw foreigners taking 'their' jobs. That said, large numbers of Central and East Europeans have in any case taken jobs in France and Germany, either illegally, or legally under EU rules such as those of the posted workers directive or national rules allowing seasonal workers in industries like agriculture. Germany now issues about half a million work permits a year to Central and East Europeans, mostly seasonal workers.

The core eurozone economies have succeeded in keeping out some of the Central and East European workers who wanted to enter, but they have failed to keep their companies at home. French and German multinationals have invested where labour is cheap, often in the new member-states. Thus for the French, enlargement means not only Polish plumbers but also *délocalisation* and the export of jobs. This has led many people to believe that enlargement is 'bad' for their countries. As argued below, enlargement has in fact been beneficial for all EU countries, but few leaders have made an effort to explain that.

[11] *Mark Leonard, 'Democracy in Europe: how the EU can survive in an age of referendums', CER, March 2006.* Politicians are finding it increasingly difficult to ignore the wishes of voters on this kind of issue. Enlargement in particular, like the EU in general, has long been a project of elites. Politicians, diplomats and experts have built the Union, with the best of intentions, over the heads of the people. That can no longer continue. The Union has entered into an age of populism, and in future both treaty changes and enlargements will require referendums.[11] Governments may wish to enlarge for 'strategic' reasons, but if they cannot persuade voters of the case for expanding the EU's borders, enlargement will not happen. Thus one *sine qua non* of future enlargement is political leadership – of the inspirational sort that has been largely lacking in Europe in recent years.

The benefits of enlargement

Caution over the pace of further enlargement is justified. But for the Union to turn its back on the whole process would be a big mistake. One of the Union's greatest successes has been to entrench democracy, prosperity, security and stability across much of the continent. Of course, there has to be a geographical limit at some point: Article 49 of the EU's Rome treaty limits membership to 'European' countries. North African countries are not in Europe and so cannot join. But for the EU to define precisely its future borders for all time would have a disastrous impact on would-be members beyond those borders.

If the EU ended talks with Turkey, hard-line Islamists and nationalists in the country would gain strength against westernisers.[12] In recent years the mutual mistrust between the moderate Islamists in the AKP government and the secularists in the armed forces and the state bureaucracy has been softened by their shared support for European integration. The removal of that goal could destabilise the political system – and lead to harmful knock-on effects on the economy. If the EU rejected Turkey there would also be strategic consequences. The lesson drawn by many in the Islamic world would be that the EU was anti-Muslim.

[12] *Charles Grant, 'Turkey, Russia and modern nationalism', CER bulletin 49, August 2006.*

However, Turkey would still be a fairly efficient and dynamic country experiencing rapid modernisation. The impact of the EU shutting the door on the Western Balkans would be much worse. Would fragile constructions such as Bosnia and Macedonia hold together? Would Serbia ever be able to swallow the bitter pill of independence for Kosovo without the prospect of EU membership for itself? If the Western Balkans is made to feel excluded from the European mainstream, economic reform and foreign investment would suffer. Endemic problems such as organised crime, corruption, ethnic tension and political violence would worsen, and could spill over into the EU.[13]

[13] *For an analysis of the current situation in the Balkans, see Tim Judah, 'The EU must keep its promise to the Western Balkans', CER essay, July 2006.*

The EU must not stint in its pursuit of Balkan enlargement. It should work to ensure that several Western Balkan states are ready to start accession talks by the beginning of the next decade. The best performers could aspire to catch up with Turkey, which has already started accession talks. Countries further afield, such as Ukraine, Moldova, Belarus and Georgia have little chance of starting talks in the foreseeable future. But if the EU said "never" to them, its ability to influence their development would be hugely weakened.

The EU should not view enlargement as a form of philanthropy. Rather, it should keep alight the flame of further enlargement for reasons of self-interest. Enlargement helps the EU to prepare itself for globalisation. The expansion of the EU into a diverse group of European economies, creating a single market of (after Bulgarian and Romanian accession) nearly 500 million people, allows more economic specialisation within the Union. The accession countries are mostly fast-growing and dynamic, offering West Europeans demand for their products, opportunities for investment and supplies of skilled labour. The East European states are now applying, more or less perfectly, EU rules on trade, investment, business regulation and competition. In fact a study by a London School of Economics researcher on the East Europeans' record of transposing EU directives into national law, and of resolving infringement cases brought by the Commission, shows that the new members on average have a better record of following EU rules than the old ones (though the Czech Republic has a particularly poor record).[14]

[14] *Ulrich Sedelmeier, 'Is there an "Eastern Problem" in the enlarged European Union?', paper presented to the 15th international conference of Europeanists, Chicago, March 2006.*

Trade and investment between the original 15 and the new ten – which had already boomed in the years leading up to enlargement – has continued to grow rapidly in the two years since they joined. Some EU countries, such as Austria and Germany, have done particularly well out of exporting to the accession countries. Many West European companies have flourished on the strength of their investments in sectors such as banking, energy, media, retail and telecoms in Central and Eastern Europe. But enlargement is also changing the EU economy in a more profound way, by allowing the emergence of a new pan-European division of labour, and so helping the EU as a whole to remain globally competitive.

Companies from France, Germany and elsewhere have reacted to globalisation by outsourcing some labour-intensive production processes to places where wages are lower. Many have chosen Central and Eastern European states, not only because of proximity but also because their business environments are increasingly similar to those of the old EU. "The relocation of production from west to east has helped Europe's companies – from cars to telecoms – to stay competitive on a global scale. Therefore, while some factory jobs may have moved to Hungary, Poland or Slovakia, many jobs in research, design and higher-value added production have been preserved or created in the old EU."[15]

[15] *Katinka Barysch, 'Enlargement two years on: economic success or political failure?' briefing note for the Confederation of Danish Industries and the Central Organisation of Industrial Employees in Denmark, April 2006.*

The benefits of enlargement are not only economic. The process enhances the security of those who live throughout the Union. Criminal gangs who traffic arms, women or drugs do not respect the EU's external frontier and stay outside. Nor do terrorists. Such groups can base themselves in relatively safe havens outside the EU, but close by, and then operate easily within the Union. The EU states' various law-enforcement agencies are better able to combat criminal and terrorist gangs that are on rather than off EU territory. Were the EU to decide that the Western Balkans should remain permanently beyond its boundaries, as a kind of black hole on the map of Europe, the many criminal gangs that operate in Western Europe from Balkan bases would be delighted. As part of the accession process, the EU helps the governments concerned to deal with security threats. Thus the EU has helped Bulgaria with its (still inadequate) efforts to tackle organised crime, for example by strengthening its police forces and border guards through the provision of better training and new equipment.

Finally, enlargement brings strategic gains. Europe's biggest problem in the multi-polar world of the 21st century will be remaining relevant. In a world where China, India, Brazil, Russia and other countries are becoming richer and more powerful, the EU needs to ensure that its voice is heard in the management of global affairs. A little Europe would have a small voice. A wider Europe, with a larger population, a stronger economy and a broader geographical extent – so long as it learns to speak with a single voice – would be a more influential pole. For example, an EU that included Turkey, Bosnia and Albania would be listened to with more respect in the Muslim world. It would stand a better chance of helping to shape the Middle East peace process.

4 Enlargement and *avant-garde* groups

If the EU's governments succeed in negotiating a revision of its treaties in the next few years, the results are likely to be modest. Many countries, and not only relatively Eurosceptic ones like Britain and Poland, will refuse to accept the big changes that 'maximalists' such as Germany, Italy and Spain will demand. The Dutch and the French, having voted No to the constitutional treaty, will oppose any change that looks like an attempt to introduce large parts of the constitution through the back door. The only kind of treaty revision that can feasibly attract 27 signatures is unlikely to satisfy those who want the EU radically transformed into some sort of 'political union'.

Furthermore, there is no guarantee that a new treaty, even one with limited provisions, will be ratified. Some countries may choose to ratify through referendums, the outcome of which can never be certain.

Whatever happens, the EU is unlikely to adopt a major new treaty, comparable to the Maastricht/Amsterdam/Nice/constitutional documents, for the remainder of the decade. And that is a problem for enlargement. With the likelihood of either no treaty-based integration, or only modest doses of it, plenty of influential politicians and officials will argue that the EU should suspend enlargement. British politicians tend not to see the inevitability of the link between deepening and widening, but others do.

EU leaders should therefore make better use of variable geometry, the idea that not every member-state need take part in every EU policy area. Already, of course, some EU countries opt out of the euro, the Schengen agreement on passport-free travel, or EU defence policy. The current treaties allow groups of member-states to move ahead in certain policy areas, under the so far unused 'enhanced co-operation procedure'. An *avant-garde* group could also emerge independently of the EU institutions: the Schengen scheme started as an inter-governmental accord, before being folded into the EU treaties in 1997.

Originally, variable geometry was viewed as something that allowed different members to move at different speeds along the same road towards the same goals. For example, the fathers of the euro assumed that the opt-outs negotiated by Britain and Denmark in 1991 and 1992 were exceptional and temporary. Thus the euro became part of the *acquis communautaire*: every new member is obliged to sign up to the principle of euro membership. Only in the last few years has it become apparent that variable geometry is allowing countries to proceed along divergent paths: Britain, Denmark and Sweden are nowhere near joining the euro, while Britain and Ireland show no signs of abolishing border controls with their EU partners. The reality is that the member-states no longer share all the same goals, and it would be surprising if 27 diverse countries did so. The fact that the current EU system does allow *avant-garde* groups and could accommodate more of them is to be welcomed. An EU that tried to force all member-states into the same box would suffer a serious loss of legitimacy in some of them.

It would be hard to deny that a wider and therefore more diverse EU will require more variable geometry. But I would go further and argue that greater use of it could help the cause of enlargement. If the countries that aspire to a political union were able to build *avant-gardes* in certain policy areas, and thus revive a sense of forward motion, they would be less likely to oppose further widening of the Union.

One of these is Belgium. Guy Verhofstadt, the Belgian prime minister, has called for the eurozone to develop into a 'political union'.

The creation of a political union makes it possible to
continue enlarging the union without any major
problems....this approach also constitutes the ideal
solution to a problem that is becoming ever more acutely
felt: the absence of an interim stage between when a
country knocks on Europe's door and when it actually
becomes a member of the Union. Provided that applicant
member-states met the required criteria, [16] *Guy Verhofstadt, 'The United*
they could always accede to the Union *States of Europe', The Federal*
without having to join immediately the *Trust/ IB Taurus, 2006.*
demanding core group.[16]

Plenty of other politicians have made the connection between
variable geometry and enlargement. "To speak of a pioneer group,
or an *avant-garde*, is to recognise that one can only reconcile a
deepening of EU integration with enlargement of the EU by
allowing some countries to go further," [17] *Jacques Delors, 'Europe needs*
wrote former Commission president *an avant-garde, but ...', CER*
Jacques Delors in 2000.[17] *bulletin 14, October 2000.*

Verhofstadt and Delors are writing about a core Europe, which I
regard – for reasons discussed below – as unlikely to emerge. But
the logic of their argument would apply just as strongly to the
emergence of a number of overlapping *avant-garde* groups, which
seems much more likely. Indeed, the current trend towards
variable geometry is unmistakable. For example, seven member-
states (Austria, the Benelux three, France, Germany and Spain)
signed the Treaty of Prüm in May 2005, a kind of super-Schengen
agreement that among other things enables the signatories to share
information on finger-prints and DNA, and to co-operate on
aircraft security and hot pursuit across borders.[18] More
informally, the interior ministers of Britain, France, Germany,
Italy, Poland and Spain – the 'G-6' – collaborate on counter-
terrorism. Meanwhile Iceland, Norway [18] *Hugo Brady, 'A new avant-*
and Switzerland, though outside the EU, *garde for internal security', CER*
have joined the Schengen agreement. And *bulletin 44, October 2005.*

then there are issue-based sub-groups of members, such as that of Britain, France and Germany – the 'EU-3' – that leads EU policy on Iran.

All these groupings promote European interests or integration. The trend for not every country to take part in every policy area should be welcomed. Any forum that has 25 or 27 governments represented around a table is seldom likely to be useful or effective.

The variable geometry envisaged here is different to the idea of a 'hard core' or 'concentric circles' that has periodically been floated not only by Delors and Verhofstadt, but also senior French politicians such as Valéry Giscard d'Estaing and Dominique Strauss-Kahn. Their idea is that France and Germany should lead a group of integrationist members into a new organisation that would establish closer co-operation across a broad range of policy areas, rather than one particular subject. Those left in the outer circle would be in the EU but not the new core. This scenario has never been very plausible, because of the institutional, political and judicial difficulties that would ensue, and because few German leaders fancy the idea. It has become even less plausible in recent years, because Franco-German leadership has gained a poor reputation among many other members, and because of the weakness of the governments in Paris and Berlin.[19]

[19] *Charles Grant, 'What happens if Britain votes no? Ten ways out of a European constitutional crisis', CER pamphlet, March 2005 (see chapter five).*

This pamphlet suggests that an alternative scenario is both plausible and desirable. This would be based on the current situation: several *avant-garde* groups, each with a different membership, would overlap.

Evidently, variable geometry – whether in the form of treaty-based enhanced co-operation, clubs established outside the treaties, or informal groups focused on particular policies – entails risks. However, most of the potential pitfalls can be dealt with.

★ *The danger of exclusion.* The British government has traditionally opposed variable geometry, fearing that if it stayed out of a group it would lose influence in the EU – and that if it later tried to join it might find the door bolted. Any *avant-garde* group should be entitled to establish entry criteria for those who wish to join. But these criteria must be interpreted in an objective manner, to ensure that a member-state is not excluded out of prejudice. The Nice treaty's provisions on enhanced co-operation give the Commission such a policing role. The countries that signed the Treaty of Prüm have said explicitly that, if their venture is a success, they will invite other member-states to sign in 2008. The problem of exclusion is more pronounced for informal groupings. When the 'EU-3' began their Iranian diplomacy, other member-states resented being left out. However, the subsequent involvement of Javier Solana, the EU's foreign policy chief, who reports back to the other governments, has reassured most of them.

★ *Avant-garde groups could weaken EU institutions.* Groups established outside the framework of the treaties, whether formal or informal, risk undermining the role of the Commission, Parliament and Court of Justice, to the extent that inter-governmental arrangements do not involve EU institutions. But precautions can be taken to ensure that such groups mesh smoothly with the institutions. For example, when the Schengen agreement was established – initially, outside the EU treaties – the Commission was invited along as an observer. The signatories of the Treaty of Prüm have taken care to ensure that it is compatible with EU law.

★ *Variable geometry is 'undemocratic'.* That is true, to the extent that neither the European nor national parliaments have oversight of inter-governmental organisations. However, *avant-garde* groups are only as undemocratic as governments choose to make them. If a group of member-states created an enhanced co-operation, the Nice treaty would give the European

Parliament a role in what it does (if the enhanced co-operation dealt with normal Community business, decisions would require the Parliament's consent; on foreign policy the Parliament would merely be informed; and on justice and home affairs it would be asked for an opinion). Other sorts of *avant-garde* grouping need not be unaccountable. Thus the president of the European Central Bank (ECB) appears before the European Parliament's monetary affairs committee (though he is not obliged to follow the wishes of MEPs). The Western European Union, a defence sub-group that has largely merged with the EU, still has its own parliamentary assembly, consisting of representatives from national parliaments. Other inter-governmental groupings could create their own systems of parliamentary oversight. As for the Treaty of Prüm, it has been ratified by the parliaments of the signatory countries, which gives it a certain legitimacy.

★ *Variable geometry could lead to the unravelling of the acquis communautaire.* The more you allow some countries to pick and choose, the greater the risk that others will demand the right to opt out of existing policies they dislike. At the time of Britain's 2005 general election, for example, the Conservatives talked of using variable geometry to pull Britain out of the common farm, fisheries and foreign policies. The EU therefore needs to define the set of policies that every member must take part in. This should include trade, competition, a set of common rules for fisheries and agriculture (though not necessarily today's Common Agricultural Policy), environmental standards, policies for helping the EU's poorer regions, the single market (including cross-border aspects of transport and energy policy), free movement, some co-operation on borders and policing, development assistance and common foreign policies. That leaves policies and institutions such as the euro and its budgetary rules, the co-ordination of tax policies (so long as that does not harm the single market), common border controls, criminal justice and defence policy, as suitable for variable geometry. The list of 'compulsory' policies proposed here is compatible with the strictures of the current treaties, with the exception of the euro: I see no value in maintaining the fiction that everyone has to join the euro.

Transitional arrangements for new members

When a country joins the EU, it is normally subject to 'transitional arrangements' that exclude it from full participation in certain policies for a number of years. Sometimes these work to the benefit of the new member: East Europeans who joined the EU in 2004 will not have to apply all the (very costly) environmental rules for up to seven years. Sometimes the transitional arrangements work, supposedly, in the interests of the old members. Thus in 2004, 12 of the old member-states insisted on limiting access to their labour markets for workers from the new member-states for up to seven years.

Most applicants naturally resist that kind of measure, unwilling to be given a status that could be seen as second-class membership. However, some applicants and future applicants should think very seriously about tolerating some long or even indefinite transitional periods. One big reason why many people worry about Turkey in the EU is that they fear its workers will take their jobs. Free movement of labour would be good for Turkey, and in most respects good for the existing member-states. But given Turkey's current poverty – with per capita GDP at around 30 per cent of the EU average – worries about Turkish immigration are understandable. Turkey should be prepared to envisage a provision that would, for example, allow a member-state to limit inflows of Turkish labour indefinitely – but only for as long as Turkey's per capita GDP was below, say, 50 per cent of the EU average.

Once Turkey had been in the Union for a few years, many member-states would probably not wish to apply such restrictions. After all, the Turkey that joins the EU, if it does, will be very different to, and much richer than, the

Turkey of today. Furthermore, given the problem of ageing societies in many EU countries, Turkey's pool of labour may start to look appealing. Some Turks would understandably view membership with limits on free movement of labour as an insult. But Turkish negotiators should, as a last resort, be prepared to accept such limits.

Similarly, some member-states might prefer a Turkey that joined the EU to stay outside some key aspects of Schengen, such as the abolition of passport controls – which is what the British and the Irish do. That would offend some Turks, but others would probably prefer their country to retain border controls.

Turkey would be much better off inside the EU, with restrictions, than outside. This situation would be a kind of variable geometry, in the sense of not every member taking part in every policy. Like the other kinds, it should make enlargement less threatening to those who fear it.

What scope for avant-garde groups?

Whenever continental European politicians talk about extending the use of flexible integration, critics of the concept – notably in the British diplomatic establishment – tend to respond: "So where is it going to happen?" They point out that for all the talk of *avant-garde* groups and variable geometry, there does not seem to have been much political will to translate words into deeds. In the summer of 2006, it is true, there is no great momentum for the establishment of new leadership groups. But that could change within a year or two. One could imagine enhanced co-operations being used for environmental policy, transport policy, education or R&D.[20]

[20] *See 'Flexibility and the European Union', Federal Trust, October 2005.*

The rest of this chapter, however, looks at the prospects of variable geometry in four areas where I believe it is most plausible: the Euro Group, corporate taxation, justice and home affairs, and defence. I devote some space to this analysis because I regard variable geometry as crucial to the future shape of the EU. I believe that if the EU does extend its use of variable geometry, it is much more likely to continue enlarging. However, readers uninterested in the feasibility of *avant-garde* groups may wish to skip to the end the chapter.

The Euro Group

In the long run, the most likely area for an extension of variable geometry is the euro. The Euro Group, consisting of the finance ministers of the euro countries, is an increasingly important institution. At the start of 2005 these finance ministers elected one of their own number, Jean-Claude Juncker, as their chairman. The group meets on the evening before the monthly sessions of Ecofin, which all 25 finance ministers may attend. It is serviced by a small secretariat based in the Commission. Those who participate in both forums report that discussions in the Euro Group are more likely to be useful and focused. The Euro Group sometimes prepares the ground for formal decisions taken by Ecofin the next day.

The Euro Group could and should develop in three ways:

★ *Surveillance of eurozone economies.* If some of the eurozone's poorly performing economies do not improve their performance, they may create problems for their partners in the euro. Neither the Commission nor Ecofin has proved very effective at putting pressure on, say, Italy and Spain to address their competitiveness problems; or at persuading Germany to boost domestic demand.[21] The Euro Group is making some efforts to improve its surveillance of national economies but should do more.

21 'Will the eurozone crack?', Simon Tilford, CER pamphlet, September 2006.

★ *Creating links between structural reform and macro-economic policy.* Jean Pisani-Ferry and André Sapir have pointed out that there is a much stronger case for eurozone members to co-ordinate their structural reforms than there is among the wider EU membership. If one member of a currency union implements reforms, there is more spill-over on fellow members than on countries outside it. Furthermore, the euro

[22] *Jean Pisani-Ferry and André Sapir, 'Last exit to Lisbon', Bruegel policy brief, March 2006.*

area could suffer from a divergence of commitment to reform among its members.[22] The Euro Group should therefore prepare its own programme of structural reforms for the euro area. The Stability and Growth Pact should be rewritten so that countries which carry out structural reforms are allowed to spend more on helping social groups disadvantaged by them. The pact's current rules do not allow for such flexibility. The Euro Group also needs to establish channels with the ECB that would allow the two institutions to bargain: the bank might be more willing to cut interest rates if the euro countries could demonstrate that they were adopting painful economic reforms. In the spring of 2006 Juncker wrote to Jean-Claude Trichet, the ECB's governor, suggesting a more structured relationship. But he did not receive a response. The ECB appears to fear that such arrangements could compromise its independence.

★ *The external representation of the eurozone.* The euro area has little meaningful external representation, except through the ECB and the governments of the euro countries. The eurozone therefore often punches below its weight in international financial discussions and negotiations. For example, neither the EU nor the eurozone is represented in institutions such as the IMF. The IMF is currently preparing to reform its governing structures, partly to give Asia greater representation. The EU countries are over-represented, with seven of the 24 seats on the IMF board (29 per cent), though they account for only about 20 per cent of world GDP. Pisani-Ferry and Sapir argue convincingly that the euro countries should seize the opportunity of the current reform process to propose a single eurozone seat, and to reduce the eurozone's votes and quotas to a size commensurate with its economic weight. That would free votes and seats for the Asian countries that are currently under-represented, and enhance their sense of ownership of the Fund. "The euro area would trade off formal, but largely ineffective, power for a formally diminished but more effective influence in world economic affairs."[23]

[23] *Jean Pisani-Ferry and André Sapir, 'Only basic reform can deliver legitimacy to the fund', Financial Times, June 5th 2006.*

Despite the compelling case for the Euro Group to develop in these kinds of way, not much is happening at the moment. Juncker has not yet established himself as a heavyweight leader – though the ECB's wariness of the institution makes his task difficult. The weakness of the French government – for decades the main champion of *gouvernement economique* in Europe – is a serious handicap to any effort to reform the Euro Group.

However, the next time France and Germany decide that they need to strengthen their own ties in ways that boost the cause of Europe, they may focus on the Euro Group. One idea – promoted among others by Wolfgang Münchau of the *Financial Times* – would be for the Euro Group to hold regular summits. For example, the heads of government of the euro countries could meet on the day before EU summits. The argument for such a forum is that only the top people in governments have the clout to take difficult decisions on, say, chastising a poorly performing member, or agreeing on a controversial set of economic reforms.

Some heads of government have suggested that the Euro Group should form the basis of a 'core Europe'– involving integration across a wide range of policy areas. One is Jacques Chirac, though so far he has been short on specifics:

> States wishing to act together in addition to the common policies should be allowed to form pioneering groups. Such groups must remain open to those wanting to join them. We did so with the euro, Schengen and defence initiatives. Likewise, Eurozone members should deepen political, economic and social integration.[24]

[24] *Jacques Chirac, 'Europe needs strength and solidarity, Financial Times, October 26th 2005.*

Guy Verfhofstadt also argues that it makes sense for the euro states to integrate more closely across a whole range of policies. He calls for "a core group within the European Union to seize the initiative…this group will consist of countries belonging to the eurozone or which at least plan to join it shortly". The reasons for making the euro the basis of a core Europe are that the currency is an established institution that works; that the criteria for joining the euro are clear, so the group could not discriminate against member-states on the outside; and that "the eurozone comprises a number of member-states that have already embraced a common destiny".

Verhofstadt calls for the euro countries to establish common policies to fight unemployment and slow growth, tackle crime, develop common legislation on minimum social standards and taxation, boost R&D, develop 'trans-European information networks', establish a common army and speak with a single voice on foreign policy. The core would be the 'United States of Europe', and those left outside it would form the 'Organisation of European States'.[25]

[25] Guy Verhofstadt, 'The United States of Europe', The Federal Trust/ IB Tauras, 2006.

However, while building up the Euro Group makes sense in policy areas that are directly linked to the euro, there is not much sense in trying to use it as the foundation of a core Europe. Any sub-group of EU members that lacked the British would be ineffective in foreign or defence policy. Nor is there any particular logic that links the euro zone to integration in justice and home affairs (Ireland is unlikely to become a full member of Schengen but is in the euro). The eurozone does not even make sense as an area for co-operation on corporate taxation, because different euro countries have very different views on the subject, and very different interests: Ireland opposes tax harmonisation and benefits from low corporate rates, while France and Germany favour harmonisation and higher rates. The extension of the eurozone into Central and Eastern Europe – starting with Slovenia in 2007 – will give Ireland plenty of allies in these arguments.

Corporate taxation

Several EU governments want to harmonise corporate tax rates, to prevent competition among member-states eroding income from business taxation. France and Germany, for example, are very critical of the low corporate tax rates operating in Ireland and parts of Central and Eastern Europe. However, EU-wide measures on company taxation require unanimity, which means that governments opposed to harmonisation of rates have always been able to block them. In any case, harmonisation of rates would in itself be meaningless, since different countries calculate company profits in different ways. Only if 'tax bases' – the definitions of what corporate income is taxable – are harmonised does it make sense to set a minimum rate.

The former internal market commissioner, Fritz Bolkestein, floated the idea of harmonising tax bases in an enhanced co-operation. Governments might support such an initiative for two reasons. One would be to promote a more efficient single market. A single method for calculating tax liabilities would make life easier for companies, and also make much clearer which countries really had onerous tax systems. It would therefore encourage governments to engage in tax competition. The second reason for supporting the harmonisation of tax bases would be as a preliminary to harmonising rates.

In January 2006 Thierry Breton, France's finance minister, declared that he was in favour of harmonising tax bases and setting a minimum rate, in an enhanced co-operation. He also claimed that he had German support for this – which remains to be seen. However, even if France, Germany and others did establish such an *avant-garde*, they would probably not be able to deal with the problem which worries them, namely tax competition from East European states. For the East Europeans would have no incentive to join such an enhanced co-operation and forego one of their attractions as a place to invest.

So if France and other relatively high-tax countries did establish an *avant-garde* that harmonised corporate tax bases and set minimum rates, they would not be able to influence tax systems elsewhere in the EU, and they could damage their own competitiveness. Yet they might still see reasons for going ahead. They could argue that an enhanced co-operation for company taxation would not deter inward investment in the countries covered. For although an investor would face a minimum rate of tax, he or she – if investing in several countries in the *avant-garde* – would also benefit from the simplicity of a single tax system throughout the area. The investor would also appreciate the relatively high level of public services likely to be offered by the countries in the enhanced co-operation.

In any case, those who doubt that France and Germany would 'shoot themselves in the foot' by harmonising corporate tax rates should not under-estimate the strength of feeling in some quarters against low tax rates elsewhere in the EU. In April 2004, Gerhard Schröder made an explicit – and unenforceable – threat to East European governments that they could lose structural funds unless they co-operated on tax. He said it was unacceptable "that Germany, as the biggest net payer, finances unfair tax competition against itself".[26] He meant that it was unfair for poorer members to use EU aid (much of it paid for by Germany) to finance tax cuts that encouraged firms to relocate from richer states to poorer ones. There is of course no connection between the EU's regional aid policies and its rules on tax. But after the next French presidential election, the winner could be

[26] *Katinka Barysch, 'Is tax competition bad?', CER bulletin 37, August 2004.*

tempted to suggest to Germany that the two countries revive the idea of an enhanced co-operation on company taxation.

Justice and home affairs
One area where an increase in variable geometry is very plausible is justice and home affairs (JHA). The Schengen agreement was a successful piece of variable geometry, conceived outside the treaties but later shifted into them. The recent treaty of Prüm suggests that more variability is on the way, as do the 'G-6' meetings of interior ministers. The constitutional treaty contained special provisions that would have allowed groups of countries to go ahead in co-operation

on criminal justice, leaving behind members that did not wish to be involved. Although those provisions are unlikely to be revived, some of the more enthusiastic governments may at some point try to press ahead – within the framework of the treaties, or outside them – with the harmonisation of criminal justice.

There is already much variable geometry in JHA co-operation. Denmark, the UK and Ireland have negotiated special arrangements, which allow them to choose which JHA policies they join. For example, the UK and Ireland have opted out of the Schengen free travel area, while opting into co-operation on policing and criminal justice. Neither they nor Denmark participate in initiatives on legal immigration. The Central and East European countries, though full participants in all JHA policies, have not yet joined the free travel area. The border controls between them and their western neighbours will not come down until the latter decide – perhaps in 2008 – that the new members have implemented the relevant *acquis*.

The EU is currently trying to achieve progress in three areas of internal security. The member-states have agreed to:

★ share all intelligence and information from their police and border services by 2008;

★ give more powers to police forces when dealing with cross-border crime;

★ and co-operate more closely on criminal justice, for example through the mutual recognition of each others' judgements on serious criminal offences.

However, the EU's momentum in all three areas is stalling. The practical difficulties of implementing the sharing of information among 25 members, each with a large number of government departments, are immense. The 2008 deadline is certain to be missed. Recent initiatives to enhance the powers of police forces that need to cross a national border have achieved nothing. There has been some progress on the third objective, with agreement on minimum sentences in areas like terrorism, human trafficking and illegal drugs; but progress is slowing down in this area too.

These difficulties led the Benelux three, Austria, France, Germany and Spain to sign the Treaty of Prüm in 2005. These seven have agreed to share some of the most sensitive sorts of information, such as DNA data, among themselves. In the summer of 2006, Italy signed the Prüm treaty and Finland said that it planned to do so. With an eighth member the group has reached the threshold required for forming an enhanced co-operation under the rules of the Nice treaty. If the Prüm governments so decide, the group could become a formal part of the EU, reassuring those who fret that *avant-gardes* outside the treaties may undermine the Union.

The Prüm group is likely to attract further members and integrate in new areas, because progress at 25 is becoming increasingly difficult in JHA. In May 2006, the Commission proposed activating Article 42 of the existing treaties. This allows the member-states – if they are unanimous – to remove national vetoes on decisions on crime and policing. But a number of governments are blocking this change.[27]

[27] *Germany is one of the countries resisting this move – despite the fact that it normally champions more majority voting. A top German official explained why: "We do not want to take any steps that would allow others to argue that the EU can work well without the constitutional treaty."*

The Prüm group could decide to move quicker than the rest of the EU on enhancing the powers of police forces to cross borders and harmonising criminal laws. If the group decided to move Prüm inside the EU treaties, it could also give the European Court the power to enforce the implementation of EU criminal justice measures in Prüm countries. Inside or outside the treaties, the group might develop a system of European bail. It could even grant national prosecutors the right to initiate a case in the courts of another group member, in cases of 'cross-border' crime.

In the autumn of 2006 the German government was talking of using its presidency (in the first half of 2007) to persuade every member to adopt Prüm. If all 25 did so, the chances of the whole EU signing up to the ambitious ideas of the preceding paragraph would be minimal. Every *avant-garde* faces a choice between faster progress and a wider membership.

Defence

Defence, too, is an area well suited to variable geometry. Already, Denmark opts out of the European Security and Defence Policy and the European Defence Agency. The EU is in the process of establishing 13 'battle groups', rapid reaction forces designed to fly to a conflict zone to stabilise it before peacekeepers arrive. Only 20 of the 25 member-states are involved in the battle groups. OCCAR, the organisation established to manage multilateral armaments programmes, has just six members: Belgium, Britain, France, Germany, Italy and Spain. Twenty-two member-states – only Denmark, Hungary and Spain staying out – have signed up to a new a new code of conduct on defence procurement. All these examples are of inter-governmental co-operation; the Nice treaty forbids enhanced co-operation in defence (though the constitutional treaty would have removed that restriction).

Given the great variety in military capabilities and ambitions among the 25, further sub-groups are likely to emerge in this area. There is already much co-operation on specific capabilities, driven by the logic that it should allow governments to save money: thus six member-states plus Turkey are collaborating on the A-400M military transport plane; Italy and Germany (with the US) are building the MEADS air defence system; and Britain and France are talking about developing some common systems for the aircraft carriers they plan to build. In the future, some member-states might decide to pool their support operations for certain sorts of equipment, or some of their logistical organisations, again with the motive of saving money (for example, the countries which lease air transport are planning to set up Salis, a single network to co-ordinate the leasing of Ukrainian and Russian transport planes).[28]

[28] Edgar Buckley, 'Britain and France should pool their defence', CER bulletin 49, August 2006.

At some point the countries with stronger capabilities may wish to organise and extend their current ad hoc co-operation into some sort of formal body. This would probably encourage joint research and procurement, and could possibly extend to the pooling of capabilities and role specialisation. The point would be to try to get governments to co-operate in ways that fit with EU goals – such as the development of particular military capabilities or forms of expertise. Such an organisation would not be credible without British participation. This should not be impossible: it was Tony Blair who, at his summit with Jacques Chirac at Le Touquet in February 2003, called for the establishment of a capabilities-based defence *avant-garde*.[29] And when in 2004 the constitutional treaty fleshed out that concept with 'structured co-operation' – the idea that member-states satisfying certain capability criteria should join an EU defence *avant-garde* – the British were supportive.

[29] Daniel Keohane, 'Europe needs an avant-garde for military capabilities', CER briefing note, April 2003.

Europe's variable future

In the coming decades the EU is likely to look much less homogeneous than it looks today. A core Europe – with a leading group of countries integrating across a broad range of policy areas – remains unlikely. But there will be increasing numbers of sub-groups, focused on particular issues or policy areas. Europe's political geography will become more complicated. *Avant-garde* groups may not emerge in exactly the ways suggested in this chapter. But I believe the most likely areas for more variable geometry are the Euro Group, company taxation, justice and home affairs, and defence.

An increasing number of policy-makers and politicians recognise this trend and see it as desirable. Nicholas Sarkozy, a probable

French presidential candidate, is one. His Friends of Europe speech, a serious analysis of the Union's institutions, is worth quoting at length.

> We need a new motor: those who wish to advance must take their responsibilities. I believe in the utility of variable geometry groups for particular subjects. I'd like to see, subject by subject, the countries that are most interested or most concerned, get together to prepare the work of the Council....it is for these states to explore new kinds of solidarity, while leaving open the possibility for others to join them; it is for them to find the legal forms to sustain their common action. Let Portugese, Greeks, Spaniards, Italians and French together makes proposals on dealing with forest fires. Let the seven countries contributing peacekeepers to Lebanon get together and support each other. Let the eurozone continue to strengthen. Let the Mediterranean countries together define the most effective measures for fighting illegal immigration.[30]
>
> 30 *Nicholas Sarkozy, speech to Friends of Europe, Brussels, September 8th 2006.*

Sarkozy, of course, is not only favourable to variable geometry, but also hostile to enlargement. Nonetheless, I believe that if his vision of multiple, overlapping *avant-gardes* became reality, advocates of enlargement would find it easier to win the argument against opponents. A country such as France, taking part in most of the leadership groups, would become more relaxed about the prospect of a country joining the EU but not the *avant-gardes*.

5 The European neighbourhood policy

If, as is likely, EU enlargement proceeds only slowly in the coming years, the Union's 'neighbourhood policy' will become increasingly important. The strategically significant but little known European neighbourhood policy (ENP) connects the EU to neighbours that are unlikely to become candidates in the foreseeable future, or unable to on account of being outside Europe.

The EU is surrounded by an arc of instability, running from Belarus in the north east, down through Ukraine and Moldava, into the Western Balkans, across the Black Sea to the Caucusus, down into the Middle East and westward into North Africa. If the Balkan states and Turkey make good progress, and if they can convince the voters of France – and perhaps other countries – that their people share European values, and that their governments work in similar ways to others in the EU, they can in the long run aspire to membership.

But other countries in the neighbourhood have little prospect of joining. Despite the mediocre performance of its governments since the 'Orange Revolution' of December 2004, Ukraine is now widely recognised as a democracy that wants closer ties to the EU. But apart from Poland and Lithuania, very few member-states are keen to see it in the Union. Moldova remains the poorest country in Europe and far from meeting the basic conditions for membership. Belarus's presidential elections in March 2006 confirmed that it is no kind of democracy. Armenia, Georgia and Azerbaijan believe themselves to be in Europe, though many Europeans would disagree. Unlike Armenia and Azerbaijan, Georgia has undergone a sort of democratic revolution and is impatient to move closer to the EU (and NATO). The countries of the Maghreb and Mashreq are not in Europe and so cannot aspire to membership.

One of the EU's top strategic priorities must be to promote political and economic reform in this neighbourhood. If the EU shuns these countries it will suffer the consequences. Many of the neighbours host problems such as high unemployment, severe poverty, ethnic conflict, civil unrest and networks of criminals, terrorists and people-traffickers. Such problems are liable to spill over into Europe.

[31] An excellent summary of the ENP is the paper by Rutger Wissels in Foreign Policy in Dialogue, volume six, issue 19, 'The new neighbourhood policy of the EU', University of Trier, July 2006.

The EU launched the European neighbourhood policy in May 2004, just at the time that ten new members joined the Union.[31] The purpose is to turn the countries of North Africa, the Middle East, the South Caucasus, and the EU's eastern hinterland into a "ring of friends". The instrument for achieving that goal is the bespoke 'action plan' that the EU negotiates with each neighbour. Action plans already exist for Israel, Jordan, Moldova, Morocco, the Palestinian Authority, Tunisia and Ukraine. Those with the three Caucasus countries are almost finished. Egypt and Lebanon are negotiating action plans with the EU. Algeria is also covered by the ENP, but has not yet begun talks on an action plan. The Commission hopes such talks will start in 2007. The ENP could be extended to Belarus, Libya and Syria – but the precondition is a legal agreement between the EU and the country concerned. Talks on an accord with Syria are blocked, while the EU currently has no plans to negotiate formal agreements with Belarus or Libya.

The EU's accession process is a proven tool for transforming problematic neighbours into stable, prosperous and well-governed countries. The EU's conundrum with the neighbourhood policy is that it cannot easily transform the countries concerned without being able to dangle the carrot of accession in front of them.

This pamphlet does not attempt to provide a definitive analysis of the strengths and weaknesses of the neighbourhood policy – other, more learned publications will doubtless do so. My own, initial view is that the ENP is a broadly sensible initiative that in some cases is achieving useful results. Overall, however, the Union has not yet solved the conundrum: the incentives offered to neighbours are not big enough to persuade them to carry out many of the far-reaching reforms they need to undertake.

Confusingly, the ENP overlaps with existing EU structures and instruments. For example, the neighbours of Eastern Europe already have partnership and co-operation agreements with the EU, while the Mediterranean countries have association agreements. The latter group is linked to the EU through the 'Barcelona process', also known as the Euro-Mediterranean Partnership. Since 1995 the Union has spent large sums of money on its Mediterranean partners and built a free trade area with them (due for completion in 2010), in return for commitments to reform. The Commission does not always succeed in explaining the respective roles of the ENP and the Barcelona process in a convincing manner. However, one difference is that the latter is a collective forum; the neighbourhood policy is purely bilateral, between the EU and the country concerned.

While the association and partnership agreements are legally binding, the action plans under the ENP are political documents. Each plan sets out over a three- or five-year period the reforms that the neighbour intends to undertake, in order to align its economic and political system with European norms; and it describes what the EU can offer in terms of trade, aid, political contacts and participation in its programmes. In the words of one Commission official, "the association and partnership agreements enable us to do things with our neighbours, but do not contain mechanisms for delivery. The action plans are tool-boxes that contain detailed planning, sequencing and deadlines."

One of the most powerful tools is 'twinning': each action plan contains provisions that enable member-states to second technical experts to the neighbour concerned for a few years. There is now a huge network of such experts in countries like Jordan, Morocco and Ukraine, paid for by the Commission, working in areas such as telecoms regulation, prosecutors' offices, customs services, and plant and animal health.

In an official document, the Commission summarises the ENP thus:

> The ENP offers partner countries a new kind of relationship with the EU, going beyond co-operation to include closer political links and an element of economic integration. In addition to these incentives it offers a stake in the internal market, support in meeting EU standards as well as assistance with reforms that will stimulate economic and social development. In turn ENP partners accept precise commitments, which can be monitored, to strengthen the rule of law, democracy and the respect for human rights, including the rights of persons belonging to minorities, to promote market-orientated economic reforms, to promote employment and social cohesion and to co-operate on key foreign policy objectives such as counter-terrorism and the proliferation of weapons of mass destruction. The ENP also helps address concerns in the EU about migration, border management, organised crime and violent radicalisation.[32]

[32] 'Implementing and promoting the European Neighbourhood Policy', European Commission, November 2005.

One weakness of the Barcelona process has been the failure of the EU to get serious about applying conditionality. The EU's association agreements with the North African states allow it to withhold aid if human rights are abused. In practice, however, the

EU has never punished miscreants: one or another member-state has always found a reason for wanting to excuse the guilty government.[33] The neighbourhood policy is supposed to get round this problem by introducing the concept of 'positive conditionality': neighbours that perform well will gain access to extra money and benefits from the EU. This saves the EU the embarrassment of having to punish poor performers.

[33] *An excellent though depressing analysis of the EU's efforts to promote democracy in the Arab countries of the Mediterranean can be found in Richard Youngs, 'Europe's flawed approach to Arab democracy', CER essay, October 2006.*

As the Commission states: "The partnership is designed in such a way as to reward progress with greater incentives and benefits, which are entirely distinct from any prospect of accession. How far and how fast each partner progresses in its relationship with the EU depends on its capacity and political will to implement the agreed priorities."[34] The Commission can now argue that it is starting to apply positive conditionality: in 2006 it found €70 million to divide between Jordan and Morocco, as a reward for their strong performance. Nonetheless conditionality and human rights remain difficult concepts for some neighbours: Egypt refuses to discuss conditionality and has held up the negotiation of its action plan by insisting that the document should not provide for the discussion of individual human rights cases.

[34] *'Implementing and promoting the European Neighbourhood Policy', European Commission, November 2005.*

Action plans in practice

Some of the action plans appear to be having a positive effect. The plans with Morocco and Moldova, for example, contain programmes for tackling illegal immigration. That means money for improving border controls, upgrading reception facilities for asylum seekers and refugees, combating illegal immigration, and building institutions that can help to ensure the governments concerned respect human rights and the rule of law. Under the action plans with Jordan, Morocco and Tunisia, EU money is being spent on forums that discuss governance, democracy and human rights. The EU and Morocco are negotiating a readmission agreement – obliging Morocco to take back emigrants who enter the EU illegally – and discussing how to modernise the Moroccan judicial system. Israel, Morocco and Ukraine have joined the EU's Galileo satellite-navigation project. Almost all the partners have said they want to join the EU's education and research networks.

The Commission regards the action plans with Morocco, Jordan and Ukraine as relatively successful. Given Ukraine's strategic importance, it is worth considering the impact of the neighbourhood policy on the country. Many Ukrainians dislike the concept of the ENP, since it has nothing to say about moving towards membership, but they welcome the action plan as a useful check-list of things that they should in any case be doing for their own benefit.

Ukraine has fulfilled a number of its action plan commitments, such as the holding of free and fair presidential and parliamentary elections, in 2004 (at the second attempt) and in 2006; maintaining a free media; co-operating with the EU border assistance mission in Transdniestria (see below); signing a memorandum of understanding on energy co-operation; and approximating some laws, standards and norms to the EU level (Ukraine, however, would probably have done many of these things without the existence of the action plan). Areas where progress still needs to be made include administrative reform, judicial reform, the fight against corruption, and the effort to improve the climate for business and investment.

The action plan was negotiated by the Kuchma-Yanukovich regime, before the Orange Revolution. The EU responded to that event by showing that the neighbourhood policy can be flexible: it came up with extra provisions that had not been in the original action plan, such as talks on an easier visa regime, the prospect of market economy status (which offers Ukraine some protection against an aggressive anti-dumping policy by the EU), and the negotiation of a free trade area once the country joins the World Trade Organisation. In 2006 Ukraine won market economy status from the EU, while talks on an easier visa regime (and the related negotiation of a readmission agreement) are due to conclude before the year is over. The EU has promised Ukraine that, provided it makes a good job of implementing the action plan, it will negotiate an 'enhanced agreement' to replace the existing partnership and co-operation agreement in 2008.

The Commission claims that, increasingly, EU member-states follow the action plans' priorities in their own bilateral assistance programmes; and that international financial institutions are using them as the basis for their own strategic agendas in the countries concerned.[35] It is also proud that its action plans with Ukraine and Moldova are making a positive contribution towards the resolution of the frozen conflict in Transdniestria. The Commission's border monitoring mission is preventing smuggling between the breakaway region of Transdniestria and Ukraine, thereby undermining the criminal interests that sustain Transdniestria and putting pressure on the region to reintegrate with Moldova.

[35] 'Implementing and promoting the European Neighbourhood Policy', European Commission, November 2005.

But despite such successes, the EU has had problems with the ENP, notably in fleshing out the promises that it has made in the action plans. Several Commission directorates-general have moved very slowly to deliver on commitments made under the ENP, pleading a lack of resources. For example, the education and culture directorate-general took a long time to organise a dedicated scholarship programme for the neighbours.

Furthermore, many of the member-states are unenthusiastic: some of those most hostile to enlargement are in no hurry to deepen ties with countries just beyond the EU's borders. Take the action plan recently negotiated with Georgia. France, the Netherlands and Spain insisted that the Commission's offer should not include the prospect of a free trade area, the possibility of discussing visa regimes or any provisions for Georgia to sign up to parts of the Common Foreign and Security Policy (CFSP). The Georgian plan is thus less generous than those negotiated with Moldova and Ukraine, which are in some ways comparable countries.

One problem is that the Commission has a poor record of communicating and explaining the policy, although it does run an ENP website.[36] Beyond the realms of Brussels, foreign policy think-tanks and foreign ministries, very few people have heard of the neighbourhood policy. That does not encourage national governments to take the policy as seriously as they should. The Commission needs to find ways of getting ministers interested in the ENP. It should emphasise, for example, that the actions plans cover politically salient issues such as migration, energy security and conflict resolution.

36 http://ec.europa.eu/world/enp/index_en.htm.

Not all the ENP's problems should be blamed on the inadequacies of the Commission or the member-states. Many of the neighbours have moved very slowly to fulfil their promises under the action plans. Moldova, for example, has written parts of its action plan into its new economic plan – but has done little to implement many of the reforms it has promised to undertake. Its government is the first to admit that it needs help with implementation.

"Money is not the most important thing," says Valeriu Ostalep, Moldava's deputy foreign minister. "The money we get from the EU's TACIS programme pays for experts who come in for a week and achieve little." He says that twinning achieves much more. Moldova currently has experts from Britain, Lithuania and Poland working in its government. "If all 25 member-states were committed to twinning we'd implement the action plan in no time." He also says Moldova needs access to more flexible financial instruments, of the sort the Balkan countries get.

There will be a new and flexible financial tool, the 'European neighbourhood and partnership instrument', starting in 2007. This will replace the funds available under Eastern Europe's TACIS and the Mediterranean countries' MEDA programmes. The EU budget settlement for the period 2007-13, agreed in December 2005, provides €12 billion for the new instrument, to be spent on the ENP countries and Russia. This compares with €8.2 billion for the same countries over the previous seven years – a 32 per cent rise after adjustment for inflation. Of the €12 billion, €1 billion will be set aside for a 'governance facility', to be spent on the neighbours with the best record on governance, thereby enhancing positive conditionality.

But a more flexible and generous financial instrument may not be enough to motivate the neighbours to reform. There is a temporal imbalance between what is required of neighbours and what is delivered to them. The neighbours must carry out reforms in the short term, but most of the promised benefits (for example an easier visa regime) are years away. "We need to do better at helping our neighbours in the short term," says a Commission official. "In 2006 Moldova and Georgia have suffered from Russia banning imports of their wine, but we could not offer to take it because wine is sensitive for the EU. Nor can we move quickly on visas: we have organised meetings on the ENP and the top officials of the countries concerned have not been able to get there because of visa problems."

Even if the EU can find a way of delivering more short-term benefits, the neighbourhood policy still suffers from a structural flaw. In the past, the prospect of accession allowed the EU to have a transformational effect on those that aspired to join. But the carrots available under the ENP do not seem appetising enough to persuade governments to embrace far-reaching economic and political reforms. The experience of Central Europe is worth recalling: motivated by the goal of accession, governments spent more than ten years pushing through the many painful reforms required by the EU.

The German government, which assumes the EU presidency in January 2007, appears to recognise the point. It is preparing to propose a new-style ENP that would integrate neighbours with EU policies in specific sectors such as energy, transport, and justice and home affairs. In the energy sector, Germany's idea would be to extend the *acquis communautaire* to neighbours (see next chapter). As far as transport is concerned, the Germans want the EU to team up with the international financial institutions to build better infrastructure in the neighbours. For JHA, the plan would be less to extend the *acquis* than to strengthen the administrative capacity of the neighbours (for example, on border controls), which could in turn make it easier for the EU to soften visa regimes.

However, this new ENP would apply only to the East European and Caucasus countries, and not to the Middle East or North Africa. Some will view the German plan as 'anti-enlargement', for it seems to bear some resemblance to the 'privileged partnership' idea floated by the likes of Austrian Chancellor Wolfgang Schüssel, and others, as an alternative to Turkish membership. The new German proposal could be seen as a kind of privileged partnership for the eastern neighbours that Germany would not want to see in the EU.

There is a long-running argument within the EU over the geographical range of the ENP. Chris Patten, who as external relations commissioner helped to invent the policy, thought that one of its purposes should be to compensate the eastern countries for being told that EU membership was not on the cards for many years. He thought the other neighbours would be well looked after by the Barcelona process. But the then Commission president, Romano Prodi, over-ruled Patten and insisted that the ENP look south as well as east. Ever since, people in countries like Ukraine and Moldova have complained that they should not be in the same bracket as North Africans, who by definition can never join the EU.

I am not convinced by the arguments of the German government or Patten. It is true that Morocco can never join the EU, while Ukraine could do so one day. But the ENP's purpose is to encourage the neighbours to adopt modernising reforms that are in their own interest, and to bring them closer to the EU, whether or not they may one day join. Its purpose is not to prepare countries for membership.

The ENP should be membership neutral. If the policy is thought to be a stepping stone to membership, it will attract much hostility from some member-states. And if it is seen as an alternative to membership, few eastern neighbours will be interested.

In any case, the countries of Eastern Europe and the Mediterranean face similar transition processes. "There are quite often more similarities between countries from opposite ends of the neighbourhood than [between countries and] their own regional neighbours," writes Rutger Wissels, the Commission official responsible for neighbourhood policy. [37] "For example Ukraine has more in common with certain reform-orientated Mediterranean countries than with its immediate neighbour Belarus."[37]

[37] 'The new neighbourhood policy of the EU', Foreign Policy in Dialogue, volume six, issue 19, University of Trier, July 2006.

The strength of the neighbourhood policy is its flexibility. Some action plans are ambitious, offering the chance of participation in a wide range of EU programmes; others, designed for neighbours at a much lower level of economic development, offer much less. Thus the ENP allows the EU to treat countries that might one day join differently from others.

The ENP has succeeded in building a fairly large coalition of support among EU governments. Austria, Germany, the Nordic countries and the new member-states care more about the eastern neighbours than the southern ones, while Mediterranean member-states take the reverse view. But both groups have been prepared to support an ENP that looks east and south, so that their own pet countries are covered. An ENP that covered only post-Soviet countries would lack a broad base of support. It is unlikely that France, Spain or Italy would support the German plan.

In any case, the problems around the EU's southern rim – including severe youth unemployment, networks of illegal migrants and jihadist terrorism – are probably greater than those on the eastern side. So the EU should not attach less importance to the southern states, or declare them second-division neighbours. The German plan, if implemented, could create such perceptions. If the EU considers carefully its long-term strategic interests, it will want to devote as much energy and effort to reform in the Muslim world as reform in the post-Soviet space.

The German government seems to have taken on board some of these arguments. In the autumn of 2006, officials in Berlin were saying that although their scheme for an enhanced neighbourhood policy should be tried out first in the east, it could be applied later on in the south. In any case, the German governement is right to consider how the ENP can be beefed up. The Commission, too, is carrying out a review of the ENP in the autumn in 2006. If the EU wishes to remain a transformational power in its neighbourhood, it will need to invent new forms of association – ones that fall short of membership but are much more appealing than the current ENP.

6 Beyond the neighbourhood policy

At the moment, among the governments of both member-states and neighbours, there is not much appetite for any kind of 'half membership'. Some – though not all – of the member-states most opposed to further enlargement are also hostile to any concept that could be seen as a stepping stone on the route to membership. Hence the insistence of France, the Netherlands and Spain that Georgia be offered only a minimal action plan as part of the European neighbourhood policy. At the same time, countries such Ukraine and Georgia, which aspire to be full members, do not want to be 'bought off' with a half-way house.

Over the coming years, however, opinions are likely to shift. Leaders in EU countries who oppose full membership for neighbours will come round to the view that the Union needs to be able to shape and influence the way they develop; and these leaders will recognise that the current neighbourhood policy is an inadequate tool for doing so. Opinion in Austria and Germany is already moving this way. Angela Merkel and other German and Austrian politicians have floated the idea of a 'privileged partnership' between the EU and Turkey, as an alternative to membership – though they have done little to spell out what that would mean. The recent German plans for the EU to offer its eastern neighbours a beefed-up ENP reflect similar thinking.

Meanwhile, politicians in places such as Chisinau, Kiev and Tblisi will come to realise that accession talks are not going to be on offer in the medium term; and that they will therefore need to look at other ways of moving closer to the EU.

The EU could and should offer the neighbours closer links through participation in a wide range of EU policies. This chapter focuses, in particular, on the prospect of enhanced ties through customs unions, free trade areas and energy communities; and then on the feasibility of neighbours joining the Common Foreign and Security Policy (CFSP).

Customs unions, free trade areas and energy communities

[38] *Carl Bildt, 'The EU needs a bolder Balkan strategy', CER bulletin 46, February 2006.*

The EU established a customs union with Turkey in 1996. This means that Turkey has adopted the EU's common external tariffs and, with some exceptions, abolished customs dues between itself and the EU (though the Commission is concerned about Turkey's failure to implement parts of the customs union). Carl Bildt has suggested that the Balkan countries follow suit by forging their own customs union with the EU.[38] The Balkan states are generally unenthusiastic, since a customs union would impair their ability to protect weak industries. However,

[39] *In external trade talks, the Commission would represent those countries tied to the EU by a customs union, to the extent that tariffs were on the agenda. Since the customs union would not cover non-tariff barriers to trade, the Commission could not speak for neighbours when such barriers were discussed.*

proponents of such a union view it as a first step towards a single market between the EU and the countries concerned, and they argue that it would make subsequent accession talks (if they happen) less onerous than they would otherwise be. In any case, a customs union could allow its members to retain some tariffs in sensitive areas for transitional periods.[39]

However, an attempt to create a customs union between the EU and the Western Balkans would be problematic, mainly because of the time it would take to negotiate. Some Commission officials fear that, because of the many exceptions that the relatively weak Balkan economies would require, the negotiation could last seven or eight years. "An attempt to create a customs union with the Balkans could detract from the accession process", argues Olli Rehn, the enlargement commissioner. "Some countries might see it as a delaying tactic. Croatia, for example, and perhaps some others, could be ready for accession before the customs union was finished." The Commission points out that the existing stabilisation and association agreements go a long way towards creating free trade between the EU and the Balkan countries, and that the Central European Free Trade Area is due to cover the whole Balkans, including Romania and Bulgaria, by the end of 2006.

A more promising idea could be a 'deep free trade area' between the EU and some of its neighbours. In a conventional free trade area (FTA), the partners abolish tariffs on trade within the area, but do not go so far as the common external tariff of a customs union. The EU has told both Russia and Ukraine that, once they are in the World Trade Organisation (and thus subject to some upper limits on the tariffs they can apply), it will be ready to negotiate FTAs with them. However, while an FTA should help to encourage trade between its members, it does nothing to address the problem of non-tariff barriers. These kinds of barrier – such as protectionist procurement rules, product standards that are designed to exclude foreign goods, or restrictions on capital movements – are often the most pernicious.

Elmar Brok, the German Christian Democrat who chairs the European Parliament's foreign affairs committee, has suggested extending the European Economic Area to others of the EU's neighbours. In the EEA, Iceland, Norway and Liechtenstein contribute to the shaping of single market rules, but do not take part in decision-taking on those rules. Once the rules are made they must follow them. However, many of the EU's poorer neighbours would not benefit greatly from full participation in the single market. Their industries are too underdeveloped to survive competition from the EU economies. They would have to adopt large parts of the *acquis communautaire*, the EU's 98,000 page rule-book, but much of it would not be particularly beneficial, and they lack the capacity to administer the EU's very detailed rules.

What would best suit some of the EU's neighbours would be a compromise between a pure free trade area, that ignores non-tariff barriers, and the EEA, which would be too bureaucratic for many relatively undeveloped countries. That is the nub of a proposal from Michael Emerson and the Centre for European Policy Studies, in a report commissioned by the Commission.[40]

[40] *Edited by Michael Emerson, 'The prospect of deep free trade between the EU and Ukraine', CEPS, 2006.*

Deep free trade could mean – in addition to free trade in goods and farm products – things such as the harmonisation or mutual recognition of technical standards; convergence on EU rules for the free trade in services; and the adoption of EU rules on competition policy, corporate governance and internal market regulation, as well as some environmental standards.

The CEPS report suggests that the EU and Ukraine should decide to focus on a few priority areas of the single market, rather than over-burden the capability of its legislature, government agencies and private sector by trying to adopt all the EU's rules. But the report implies that Ukraine is not yet ready for even a limited deep free trade area. "The most important barriers to trade and investment remaining after WTO accession will be the well-known problems of economic governance (lack of transparency in business relations, lack of predictability in government policies and pervasive corruption)." A deep free trade area ('FTA+') only makes sense if Ukraine makes major strides to improve its governance. As the report notes: "The main strategic requirement for an FTA+ to become strongly beneficial is for Ukraine to switch to a transparent, consistent and largely de-corrupted regime of economic governance, and therefore to acquire a reputation for these qualities in the eyes of the international business community."

Ukraine's political classes have not covered themselves in glory since the Orange Revolution. Political turmoil has distracted them from a reform agenda. After parliamentary elections in March 2006 it took the parties more than four months to form a coalition government.

But in the long term, hopefully, Ukraine's political system will stabilise. Ukraine is probably more likely to pursue a reforming agenda if it knows that it can aspire to a goal such as deep free trade. The commission plans to include the idea of a deep free trade area in the 'enhanced agreement' that it is due to negotiate with Ukraine.

In the field of energy, the Union is already experimenting with binding its neighbours into EU policies. In October 2005, the 25 member-states, Bulgaria, Romania and the countries of the Western Balkans signed the Energy Community South East Europe Treaty. The purpose is to establish a regional energy market for gas, petroleum products and electricity, and to integrate it with the EU's internal market. It sets out a roadmap for the adoption of the EU *acquis*, thus anticipating part of the accession process. The World Bank has granted a $1 billion loan to help the establishment of the Energy Community. The treaty is being ratified by its signatory governments in the course of 2006. The energy ministers of the members will meet every six months, a secretariat is being established in Vienna, and a regulatory board will be based in Athens.

Currently, however, the EU's *acquis* in energy is rather limited. There are rules on transit, fair competition, the separation of grid and supply, access to infrastructure and some environmental issues. If all goes according to plan, the members of the Energy Community will have liberalised their markets for non-household customers by 2008, reduced the sulphur content of certain fuels by 2012, liberalised markets for all consumers by 2015 and limited the emissions of certain industrial pollutants by 2018.

As yet the EU has no rules that would oblige countries to share energy with those suffering from shortages. But there is currently much discussion on the feasibility of forging more common energy policies.[41] If these bear fruit, the Energy Community

[41] 'Green paper: A European strategy for sustainable, competitive and secure energy', European Commission, March 2006. See also the forthcoming CER paper on EU energy policy, by Katinka Barysch and Vendeline von Bredow.

will become more significant. It could also extend beyond the Balkans. The Commission's March 2006 energy green paper suggests that the Energy Community should embrace Norway, a major gas exporter, already in the European Economic Area; and Turkey and Ukraine – both countries with huge strategic importance for the transit of energy to the EU. Ukraine says that it wishes to join, though Turkey has so far turned its back on the Energy Community. The forthcoming German presidency of the EU will do its best to sustain the Energy Community and extend it into the neighbourhood.

Security partnerships

The EU should think seriously about offering some of its neighbours the chance to participate in the Common Foreign and Security Policy. I owe this idea to Salome Zurabashvili, the former Georgian foreign minister. She told me (in September 2005) that while Georgia was not yet ready for the rigours of the single market, it would benefit hugely from being part of EU foreign policy. As far as she was concerned, Georgian involvement in the CFSP would bring with it an implicit security guarantee.

She is right that it would be relatively easy for neighbours such as Georgia to subscribe to that part of the *acquis communautaire* which covers foreign policy. Adopting policies and declarations is much easier than enacting and enforcing laws – politically and technically. Candidate countries often find the implementation of EU law politically painful. But to align a country's foreign policy with that of the EU is seldom sensitive, and requires little technical capacity. That is why, during accession negotiations, one of the first chapters to be opened is usually that covering CFSP.

However, EU foreign policy is in part an expression of the values that Europeans hold in common. Therefore the EU should not try to involve a neighbour in the CFSP unless it has established a strong track-record as a working liberal democracy.

Suppose that in the next few years Georgia, Morocco and Ukraine make good progress with political and economic reform. Suppose that they earn a good reputation for respecting human rights, the rule of law, minority rights, media freedom and the independence of the judiciary. Suppose that the EU then asks them to become associates of the CFSP, with the title 'security partners'. How might this work in practice?

The EU governments and the security partner would agree that, on certain foreign policy subjects, they shared common interests. Each security partner would then send a small team of diplomats to be based in the Council of Ministers' Justus Lipsius building in Brussels. When the EU discussed one of the relevant subjects, the security partner would be asked to join in. Its diplomats would attend the relevant working groups and committees. The security partner would send a senior diplomat to the Political and Security Committee (the key Brussels committee for the CFSP), and its foreign minister to the General Affairs and External Relations Council – but only when the agenda included a topic covered by the security partnership. So the partner would help to shape some EU policies. However, not being a member, the partner would have to leave the room when the EU took a decision. When the member-states had decided on a common policy, the security partner would have the right to sign up to it – or not.

Security partnerships should not be just about procedures and institutions. The point should be for the EU and its partners to help each other deal with real problems. The flow of benefits should not be one-way, from the EU to the partners, but in both directions. For example, neighbours might help the EU to stabilise some of the very problematic regions that adjoin it.

Suitable areas for collaboration between the EU and its security partners could include, for example, the Balkans, the Caucasus, counter-terrorism, non-proliferation, the Middle East peace process and illegal immigration from North Africa. The partnership should also extend to the European Security and Defence Policy (ESDP). Already, some countries in the ENP send personnel to take part in ESDP operations: Ukraine has contributed to the EU police missions in Bosnia and Macedonia, while Morocco has sent troops to the EUFOR peacekeeping force in Bosnia. Security partners should be encouraged not only to send troops and other essential personnel to ESDP operations, but also to take part in their management.

This kind of link to the EU would probably have a beneficial impact on the neighbours concerned. Their diplomats would learn how the EU made policy. Their governments would be socialised into European ways of working. The model proposed is very different to that of the NATO-Russia council, which treats the NATO countries and Russia as two distinct entities. Security partnerships would aim to integrate neighbours into EU foreign policy, as a way of bringing them closer to the EU more generally. Evidently, this form of associate membership would make more impact on political elites than on the wider public.

The EU should not restrict security partnerships to poorer neighbours. Norway, a member of the EEA, has at various times expressed an interest in joining the CFSP. But it has been rebuffed, on the grounds that, as a country that has (twice) decided not to join the EU, it should not be allowed to 'pick and choose' from the EU's menu. But if Norway were to renew its drive to join the CFSP, the EU should not spurn it. Norway brings great expertise in certain areas of foreign policy, having played a crucial diplomatic role in the Middle Eastern and Sri Lankan peace processes. Similarly, if Switzerland was interested in the idea of a security partnership, the EU should welcome it.

I have floated the idea of security partnerships to a number of practitioners and experts, and heard several criticisms.

Security partnerships would harm the effectiveness of the CFSP machinery. The EU finds it difficult enough to forge effective policies with 25 officials or ministers sitting round the table, say many Brussels officials; with half a dozen extra seats, there would be a risk of gridlock. In fact, the rise in the number of governments around the table since May 2004 has not made it much harder to forge common policies, at least most of the time. But there is clearly a risk that the decision-making process could suffer from a growing number of participants.

Therefore, it would be wise for the EU and its partners to start off by working together on only a limited range of issues. If the EU did find the partners a drag on the chosen subjects, it would have the right to press ahead and take its own decisions on policy. Conversely, if the partners found that their views were disregarded, and that their presence was merely token, they could pull out of discussions on a particular subject. Security partners would be free to resign from that status. The EU should also retain the right to end the arrangement with the country concerned. However, if the security partnerships worked well in a limited number of areas, the EU and its partners would probably want to extend the scheme to cover more topics.

Security partnerships would create problems for the EU's relations with countries that are candidates for membership. The scheme outlined in this section would make the security partners more intimately involved in the CFSP's institutions than are current candidates such as Croatia and Turkey (Bulgaria and Romania, having signed accession treaties, are allowed to take part in EU meetings). Candidates have the right to associate themselves with EU foreign policy, but they do not have diplomats in the CFSP machinery. Turkey chooses not to align its foreign policy with that of the EU, though Ukraine and Moldova, which are not candidates, sign up to almost all EU foreign policy, using a provision in their action plans which allows them to do so. Ukraine and Moldava, however, do not take part in the discussions which lead up to the making of EU policy.

The security partnership scheme should be offered to candidates for full membership; that in itself could have a positive impact on their preparations for accession. However, the fragmentation of the Western Balkans means that there are likely to be many small candidate countries without a great deal to contribute to the broader CFSP. The EU's discussions on CFSP might become bogged down if too many countries took part.

So the security partnership concept should remain bespoke: the EU members might decide that on subject A, a particular country could contribute a lot and should be invited into the CFSP, but that on subject B it had little to add and should not be invited to join. The bigger, strategically important countries, such as Turkey, Morocco, Ukraine and Georgia, are more likely to be able to contribute to the CFSP than, say, Montenegro or Macedonia. The other criterion for inclusion in the CFSP – applying to neighbours or candidate countries – must be performance. Those countries that succeed in carrying out reforms, establishing good track records on governance, and developing friendly relations with the EU would be suitable candidates for security partnerships.

Security partnership would fail to deter neighbours from applying for membership. Jacques Delors designed the European Economic Area to deter EFTA countries from seeking EU membership, but most of them tried to become full members as soon as the EEA was in place. However, the purpose of security partnerships would not be to deter neighbours from applying, but rather to encourage mutually beneficial co-operation. Neighbours would be free to apply for membership, although if they did they would most likely be rejected. The true choice facing most neighbours would be no membership or some sort of associate membership. Faced with that choice, some neighbours may in the long run prefer the latter. If a majority of member-states suddenly started campaigning for full Ukrainian membership, the government in Kiev would of course have few incentives to join the CFSP. But in the current climate that seems unlikely.

Security partnerships would create problems for the EU's relations with Russia. Russia would probably not be pleased to see the EU extending its foreign policy into their common neighbourhood. In recent years it has taken an increasingly negative view of the EU, including its foreign and defence policies. However, Russia believes that NATO enlargement into Georgia and Ukraine would be very damaging to its interests, and it would probably view an extension of the CFSP as less threatening, given that the US is not part of it.

Today, Russian foreign policy seems to have little in common with the CFSP. But in the very long run, it is not impossible that Russia may become a truer democracy and a better respecter of civil liberties than it is today. The EU should therefore tell Russia that it too could aspire to be a security partner.

Some analysts will argue that member-states such as Poland and Latvia would never agree to such an embrace of Russia. But that depends on the long-term evolution of Russia. It is up to Russia to behave in ways that gain the confidence of EU member-states. The same analysts will also argue that Russia would never want to tie its foreign policy to that of the EU. Today, of course, Russia is too proud to want to be treated in the same way as Ukraine and Georgia. But it is not inconceivable that one day Russia might see participation in a broader CFSP as a way of helping it to build friendly relations with its neighbours. If the EU could extend the CFSP across the entire continent, its members and Russia and the countries between them would probably all get along better. However, such a happy prospect is probably decades away.

Security partnerships must be 'membership neutral'

Despite the above criticisms of the security partnership scheme, I believe that something similar to it – if not the precise model outlined here – will move up the agenda in the coming years. Having bounced the idea off a number of politicians, I have found broad support from figures such as Chris Patten, Elmar Brok, Pierre Lellouche (chairman of the NATO parliamentary assembly) and Strobe Talbott (former US deputy secretary of state).

The concept of security partnerships, like the various forms of economic association described earlier in this chapter, can only work if viewed as 'membership neutral'. The scheme must appeal to neighbours which hope that one day they will become full members, and to existing member-states which are determined that those same neighbours should not become full members. Neighbours will see it as a stepping stone to membership and several current members as an alternative.

In time, depending on how the security partners perform, some current members may rethink their opposition to the offer of full membership. Equally, the experience of security partnerships could lead some neighbours to decide that they would prefer to remain sovereign and independent, rather than join the EU.

7 Conclusion: How to revive enlargement

The current political climate in Europe is extremely hostile to further enlargement. At the time of writing, an observer could plausibly argue that Turkey's accession talks will collapse before the end of 2006; that Serbia will react to the independence of Kosovo by choosing an ultra-nationalist government that turns its back on the EU; and even that Croatia will be the last country to ever join the EU, because of the French constitutional change requiring referendums on the membership of subsequent applicants. The conclusions of the June 2006 European Council, with their reference to absorption capacity, have sent a shiver through the hearts of politicians in countries that are keen to join. This sombre climate has already had an adverse effect on the reform process in some neighbours, such as Serbia and Turkey.

But climates change. The 2010s may offer a more benign environment for enlargement than the current period. To quote an unpublished paper by my colleague Katinka Barysch:

> It seems possible that attitudes towards enlargement remain fluid, are influenced by factors that have little to do with enlargement – such as economic growth – and are based partly on a lack of information about enlargement. So one may conclude that a concerted effort by EU politicians and other opinion-formers could help to increase public support for enlargement.

In any case, whatever the level of hostility or support for enlargement among the peoples and governments of the EU, one long-term trend is unlikely to be affected. The frontiers of the EU will become fuzzier. There will still be a club called the EU, to which countries will either belong or not. But in the future political geography of Europe, there will be many gradations of integration among EU members and their neighbours.

As argued in this pamphlet, there is likely to be more variable geometry within the EU. The combination of strong leaders in France and Germany could lead to a renewed effort to build closer economic co-operation in the eurozone. The signatories of the Prüm treaty could take in more members and extend its ambit to new areas of judicial co-operation. New leaders in London and Paris might take fresh initiatives in defence co-operation, as a means of both saving money and enhancing Europe's military capabilities. Some countries may join the Union with indefinite restrictions on the application of some EU policies, such as free movement of labour. Others may join without the right to take part in certain EU policies until they can demonstrate their competence in the area concerned. Thus in September 2006, the Commission told Bulgaria that unless it made a better job reforming its judiciary, other members could resort to refusing to recognise its courts decisions. In the long term it is not impossible to imagine that Iceland and Norway – already full members of Schengen – will adopt the euro without joining the EU.

Meanwhile, some of the EU's neighbours may move much closer to it, even on the basis of the current neighbourhood policy. Israel's action plan, for example, holds out the possibility of its joining a very wide array of EU programmes. But unless the enlargement process suddenly starts to speed up – which seems unlikely – political leaders within and without the EU will start to look for new ways of linking the Union to its neighbours. Governments inside the Union – even those hostile to further enlargement – will come round to the view that the EU needs to be able to brandish bigger and better carrots, if it wishes to influence its neighbours. And even those neighbours that would prefer to be members will in the end welcome new forms of association as better than nothing.

The mechanisms designed to bring about closer ties could include the ideas discussed in the previous chapter, such as deep free trade areas, energy communities and participation in the CFSP.

The forging of new kinds of link between the EU and its neighbours in no way precludes further enlargement of the Union, when the climate is propitious. In the long run, enlargement could revive, so long as certain preconditions, described in the earlier chapters of this pamphlet, are met. These include:

★ *An inspired political leadership that can convince electorates of the merits of enlargement.* EU leaders should explain to voters that extending the single market and good governance across the continent enhances their prosperity and security. Sadly, there are currently few eloquent advocates of enlargement. Tony Blair is one, but he will soon be gone. The present commissioner for enlargement, Olli Rehn, provides thoughtful analyses of the benefits of enlargement, but his voice carries less weight than that of some heads of government.

★ *An avoidance of over-hasty enlargement into countries that are not yet ready.* If the EU lets in countries that are ill-prepared for membership, as it has sometimes done, enlargement may earn a bad name. However, given the current hostility to enlargement across much of Europe, this is unlikely to be a problem in the forseeable future.

★ *A healthy European economy that would make workers in existing EU members less fearful of change.* As long as millions of Europeans are unemployed, or fear for their jobs, they will naturally be reluctant to welcome new EU members and their workers. Stronger economic growth in countries such as France, Germany and Italy would lead to greater self-confidence and less fear of immigration. As Luxembourg's prime minister, Jean-Claude Juncker, has many times remarked, Europe's leaders know what economic reforms are required in order to revive the EU economy, but they don't

[42] Aurore Wanlin, 'The Lisbon scorecard VI: Will Europe's economy rise again?', CER pamphlet, March 2006.

know how to apply the reforms and then win an election afterwards. Europe's economic woes are beyond the scope of this pamphlet, but are described well elsewhere.[42]

★ *A more legitimate EU that would make people less hostile to an extension of its borders.* So long as the EU is unpopular, the idea of enlargement – extending the EU's territory – is likely to be unpopular too: enlargement is perceived as 'more' EU. Greater success for the European economies would help to revive the Union's legitimacy. But the EU also needs to develop projects and strategies that show how it can be of real benefit to the people of Europe. Discussions about treaty change, though much needed, are a turn-off for most Europeans. If the EU could pick up and run with some of the ideas developed at the October 2005 Hampton Court summit – such as creating a common energy policy, improving European universities, providing special help for those who lose from globalisation, or boosting the EU role in R&D – it

[43] 'EU 2010: A programme for reform', CER , March 2006.

[44] 'A citizens' agenda: delivering results for Europe', European Commission', May 2006.

would stand a chance of reducing its unpopularity. The EU can do a lot to make its institutions and policies work better, without changing the treaties.[43] A recent document from the European Commission seems to recognise this point.[44]

★ *An impressive performance by would-be members, to assuage the fears of those who oppose enlargement.* The best conceivable advocates of further enlargement are the countries which want join. The candidates will have to convince not only the politicians but also the voters of the existing members that they deserve to join. The faster the candidates can reform their judiciaries, stamp out corruption, welcome foreign investment, cut back state aid, respect minority rights, adopt the EU's single-market rules, and so on, the sooner they will win over hearts and minds within the EU. The candidates need not only to reform but also to think through how they present their reforms, paying a great deal of attention to public relations (Turkey, for example, has had a poor track record in public relations).[45] The applicants should also be willing to accept long or possibly indefinite transition periods that would postpone their full participation in some EU policies. That would make enlargement more palatable for some doubters.

[45] *Katinka Barysch, 'Some advice for Turkey', CER bulletin 45, December 2005.*

★ *An increase in the use of variable geometry, whether through the enhanced co-operation rules of the current treaties, or inter-governmental groups outside the treaties.* If the most integrationist member-states were able to move ahead in *avant-garde* groups in certain areas – for example, in taxation, judicial co-operation, the economic management of the eurozone, or defence – some people would be less hostile to enlargement.

★ *Successful reform of the EU institutions, to reassure those who fear that enlargement will weaken them.* Though a dull subject that does little to inspire electorates, institutional reform is nonetheless essential. The EU cannot get larger and larger without changing the way it operates. Some meaningful changes could be implemented without changing the treaties, notably in the area of foreign policy.[46] But other reforms will require amendments to the treaties. Many EU governments are planning another attempt to revise the treaties in 2007. Advocates of enlargement should welcome an 'inter-governmental conference' for that purpose. For if the EU were to shy away from treaty change, for whatever reason, the prospect of it taking in any countries after Croatia would become very bleak. Many governments would simply block further enlargement.

[46] *Charles Grant and Mark Leonard, 'How to strengthen EU foreign policy', CER policy brief, May 2006.*

And that would be regrettable. Enlargement gives the EU not only more influence over its immediate neighbourhood, but also more weight in the wider world. A Union that covered the entire continent – including a few Muslim countries – would have a larger and more successful economy, and stand a better chance of holding its own in negotiations with emerging economic super-powers. It would have a bigger voice not only in the Middle East but also across the globe. If, after the accession of Croatia, the EU builds a wall around itself, we will be left with a little Europe in every sense.

★